WAR FACTORY

The Cresset Library

The Best Circles
Leonore Davidoff

Britain by Mass-Observation
Arranged and written by Tom Harrisson and Charles Madge

Byron: A Portrait
Leslie A. Marchand

China: A Short Cultural History
C. P. Fitzgerald

A Farmer's Year
H. Rider Haggard

The General Strike
Julian Symons

The Home Front
E. Sylvia Pankhurst

Ishi in Two Worlds
Theodora Kroeber

Japan: A Short Cultural History
G. B. Sansom

From Ploughtail to Parliament: An autobiography
Joseph Arch

The Making of the Middle Ages
R. W. Southern

The Pub and the People
Mass-Observation

A Short History of Ireland
J. C. Beckett

It Takes a Thief: The life and times of Jonathan Wild
Gerald Howson

War Factory
Mass-Observation

Wittgenstein
W. W. Bartley III

Cover: A Munitions Factory by Frederick Elwell
Reproduced by courtesy of the Imperial War Museum

WAR FACTORY

MASS-OBSERVATION

New preface by Celia Fremlin
New introduction by Dorothy Sheridan

THE CRESSET LIBRARY

London Melbourne Sydney Auckland Johannesburg

The Cresset Library

An imprint of Century Hutchinson Ltd

62–65 Chandos Place, London WC2N 4NW

Century Hutchinson Australia Pty Ltd
P O Box 496, 16–22 Church Street, Hawthorn,
Victoria 3122, Australia

Century Hutchinson New Zealand Ltd
P O Box 40–086, Glenfield, Auckland 10
New Zealand

Century Hutchinson South Africa (Pty) Ltd
P O Box 337, Berglvei 2012, South Africa

First published 1943

This edition first published 1987

Made and printed in Great Britain by
Richard Clay Ltd, Bungay, Suffolk

For

LORD HORDER

a true friend to initiative and youthful enterprise, with gratitude.

Note: In this book income levels ("class") are indicated by a simple code, thus:

A Rich people.
B "The Middle Classes".
C Artisans and skilled workers.
D Unskilled workers and the least economically or educationally trained third of our people.

CONTENTS

PREFACE
TO THE CRESSET LIBRARY EDITION

Early in 1942 I became liable for call-up with my age-group (27). During the previous three years I had been working on and off for Mass-Observation, first as a volunteer in my spare time, and latterly—after Tom Harrisson had managed to get some kind of financial support from the Ministry of Information—as a full-time Observer and interviewer.

My call-up came as no surprise—I had been expecting it, actually, for some months, and, as in the case of most women, I could have opted for some other kind of war service if I had wished—in the ATS, for instance, or the WAAF, or the WRENs. I had no objection to any of these prospects, but I thought it would be more interesting to leave the whole thing to chance, to go wherever I was sent, and try to make the most of the experience whatever it might turn out to be.

Thus it happened that I found myself in this small factory in Wiltshire, working as an unskilled hand in the machine shop.

I learned later that this posting was not as random as I had supposed it to be at the time. Apparently Tom Harrisson had pulled various strings to get me sent to a factory where he had reason to suppose the management would be interested in an M-O report. This I did not know; Tom could be very secretive with us Observers, feeling—perhaps rightly—that if we knew too much about what we were supposed to be finding out, this could have biased our attitudes and selection of material.

Be that as it may, I entered the factory just like any other of the conscripts, though with a very clear plan as to how I meant to use the experience; I was going to observe and record my findings in as much detail as I possibly could, and send my reports weekly to Tom Harrisson for the M-O files. This would have been my intention *wherever* I had been sent; this was something that we in M-O were totally committed to—to sieze on whatever experiences the war put in our way, and to record them as fully and accurately as the circumstances allowed.

I was aware, of course, of the difficulties that would be involved in making notes concurrently with actually doing the job. The problem was twofold: first, to find the time to make notes at all while working a

12-hour day with few breaks; second, to make these notes in such a way as not to arouse suspicion among my fellow-workers. When I say 'suspicion', I don't mean that I thought I was doing any harm to anybody—on the contrary, I felt that what I was doing could not fail to be beneficial to all concerned. What I was afraid of was that once the girls knew that this sort of record was being kept, all spontaneity would go out of their behaviour in my presence. Some would resent being 'spied on', and imagine that I was running to the management with tales of misbehaviour; others might glory in this novel form of extra attention, and would start showing-off. Either way, the whole thing would become stilted and artificial to the last degree.

So I had to improvise various techniques for making my record as inconspicuously as possible. By that time, I had perfected my own personal brand of speedwriting, which was a great asset; and I relied quite a bit on the short-term memorizing of lively bits of conversation. But the device I found most useful of all was that of establishing a reputation as an almost obsessional letter-writer. Using a writing-pad perched on my knee during tea-breaks and slack periods, I would start the page with 'Dear Aunt Emma' or 'Dear Sammy', or whatever, and proceed to record dialogue as continuous prose, without capitals, punctuation or quotation marks, which renders it almost unintelligible to the casual glance. And anyway, casual glances were extremely rare; my companions were far more interested in their own affairs than in my interminable letters home.

Of course, there is no method at all which enables one to get down more than a tiny proportion of the day's conversation; but provided the bits you *do* get down are not selected on the basis of any particular bias, I think the all-round picture presented will be valid.

Had I known at the time that my reports were going to land up with the factory management and not just with Mass-Observation I might have felt rather more uneasy; but I don't think that even so I would have been deterred from the project. As I said earlier, nothing I reported could have got any individual girl into trouble—the names were all scrambled; and as to any all-over lessons to be learned from the survey, these would all have been conducive to improving the lot of the workers, not to worsening it.

In any case, this all seemed to me to be of only passing significance in comparison with the historical perspective within which M-O was operating. I felt we were providing unique material for future historians. I still do. How exciting it would be if we had a record of the Trojan war through the eyes of an ordinary housewife or trader within those walls, and not solely through the eyes of warrior-kings and heroes, as interpreted by tragic poets.

Something like this, in a small way, is what we in Mass-Observation are hoping to leave to the historians of centuries ahead.

Celia Fremlin
1987

INTRODUCTION
TO THE CRESSET LIBRARY EDITION

When *War Factory* was first published in October 1943 it was given a warm welcome by the press. Women war workers were indisputably newsworthy, particularly when they were said to display an alarming lack of enthusiasm for the war effort. The *New Statesman* described the book as the 'first coherent and serious study' of a wartime industrial community lodged in the middle of the countryside. The *Guardian* called it 'a remarkable study', the *Sunday Times*, 'a fascinating examination'. Almost without exception the reviewers were happy to accept the basis on which the study was carried out and were impressed by its findings. The *Daily Herald* commented 'the girls were grossly—and it would seem, indefensibly—overworked' and goes on:

> No doubt there will be a lot of argument . . . when this book is read—as it ought to be—by the managements and workers in the production line. What is certain is that those who are responsible for maintaining the rhythm of war production in the fifth year of war will find no adequate solution of the problem of war-weariness if they ignore the penetrating human facts which are brought to light in such investigations as are recorded in this important book.

Not all Mass-Observation publications (and this one was the eleventh to appear) had received such fulsome praise. The tone of the reception must have been especially gratifying for Mass-Observation in view of the fact that *War Factory* was the work of just one Mass-Observer and was based entirely on a participant observation study. Mass-Observation had always championed the value of qualitative social research, and Tom Harrisson, the Director of M-O at this time, argues the case quite vehemently in the opening section of the book. Even by its own standards, however, *War Factory* must be seen as a highly subjective piece of work, with all the weaknesses and strengths that such an approach entails.

The Mass-Observation investigator described mysteriously in the book as a 'highly trained and experienced Cambridge graduate' was Celia Fremlin. It is typical of Mass-Observation style that we learn very little about her from the book itself. No doubt this is partly due to the hush-hush nature of the work. The factory specialized in the highly secret production of radio-location systems (radar) first used by coastal stations and later developed for RAF night fighters and the Fleet Air Arm. Security reasons alone, however, do not account for the invisibility of the investigator. It was a consequence of M-O's determined pursuit of 'objectivity'. Such anonymity would not, I suspect, be acceptable in ethnographic research today. We hear how she adjusted to the monotony of the work, but we don't know how she managed to make notes at the same time as working, for example, or how the other women responded to her (presumably) conspicuous upper middle-class background. Nor do we know how she managed to work and still make arrangements to have her small baby cared for, a problem which she shared with at least one other woman in the factory.

From other sources we know that after graduating, Celia Fremlin had taken a number of jobs in domestic service and had written up her experiences in a book called *Seven Chars of Chelsea*. This was the beginning of a career as both a writer and independent researcher spanning the last fifty years, during which her time with Mass-Observation was a brief but by no means insignificant interlude. She was recruited to Mass-Observation's ranks by Tom Harrisson just before the outbreak of war in 1939. Harrisson was understandably intrigued by someone whose interests were not dissimilar to his own—he had been working in a cotton mill in Bolton immediately before joining forces with Charles Madge and Humphrey Jennings to found Mass-Observation in 1937. Celia Fremlin soon proved herself to be one of M-O's most intrepid investigators, particularly during the London blitz when, for some of the time, she combined her observation work with employment as a waitress at the Lyons Corner Cafe. She took part in most of M-O's projects during the early war years and was closely involved in the study of morale and wartime production between 1940 and 1941 (published as *People in Production* in 1942).

She was therefore no stranger to factory life when she presented herself for duty at 'war factory' on 7 February 1942. Her placement had been arranged by the Ministry of Labour and appeared on the surface to be a straightforward conscription into war work. However, the idea of inviting Mass-Observation to study the situation had come from the factory manager, Mr Lipman. Lipman regarded himself (with some justification) as a progressive in the field of labour relations, and because he was concerned about the low level of morale among the women workers, he felt duty bound to investigate the problem properly. Celia Fremlin was therefore employed as if she had been an ordinary factory worker. Only two or three members of the management knew of her undercover role.

The factory was situated on the River Avon, a few miles outside Malmesbury in Gloucestershire. A large country house set in 14 acres of land was taken over in August 1939 and rapidly converted to meet the new requirements. Senior personnel and technical staff were poached from the Ekco factory at Southend-on-Sea, but the majority of the manual workers (chiefly women) were recruited from the surrounding area in the early months of the war. When the Ministry of Supply closed down a local textile factory, its 200 employees were taken over by the new factory. Apart from these workers, most of the recruits were unaccustomed to industrial work; either they were from farming families or they had previously been employed in domestic service, often as stable hands, maids and cooks. As the factory expanded, the urgent need for womenpower increased and conscripts were drawn in from other industrial areas.

The conscription of women was announced in Parliament in December 1941 only two months before Celia Fremlin arrived in Malmesbury. A survey undertaken for the government in mid-1941 had reported that shortages in labour power were becoming serious. The Minister of Labour, Ernest Bevin, was a staunch advocate of the voluntary principle; he hoped that enough women would take on essential war work without being compelled. No other country, even Germany, had resorted to the conscription of women and the government was reluctant to take such a step. The Cabinet was especially concerned about how *men* would feel. However, it became increasingly apparent that women (for a variety of reasons, some of which immediately become obvious after reading *War Factory*) were not volunteering in sufficient numbers and that some form of compulsion was necessary if the state's military needs were to be met. The National Service (No.2) Act which came into operation on 18 December 1941 affected unmarried women between the ages of 20 and 30. Subsequent legislation extended the age limit until by 1943, unmarried women under 50 were called up. 'Mobile' women were identified, that is, women who could, according to the government, be shifted about the country without too much domestic disruption in order to meet labour shortages where they arose. Many of the conscripts working with Celia Fremlin were young 'mobile' women eking out temporary lives in the billets and hostels of Malmesbury, the greater part of their days spent on monotonous, repetitive work requiring from them a minimum of attention, let alone initiative or involvement.

One of Celia Fremlin's most insightful and persuasive conclusions was that the low morale was significantly related both to the horrifically long shifts and to the absence of any opportunity to engage in collective, responsible and meaningful work. It is extraordinary, then, that the works manager persisted in his belief that the problem was one of propaganda. In his appendix, he writes:

> What appears to be wanted is a National consciousness that is part of the greater whole, that each has a definite stake in winning the war, and that every person, however indirectly connected with the War Effort, is part of an essential War machine.

Had he added an *equal* stake he might have begun to address the problem (women's rates of pay, for example, were well below those of the men's). Here was a typical wartime situation where women were uprooted from their communities and forced into menial, unsatisfying work, where their social and cultural needs were neglected, where there was little prospect of promotion, adventure or social recognition and where everyone, management and workforce alike, regarded the whole situation as transient. There is a current tendency to romanticize women's experience of the Second World War, to invoke heroic images of women at the wheels of tractors or 'manning' anti-aircraft guns. *War Factory* provides a useful corrective. For women like Celia Fremlin, the war certainly did provide constant challenges and ones which she was fortunately able to meet; for Hilda, Peggy, Edith and all the other women described in *War Factory*, the war was less of a thrill. It would be interesting now to see whether any of the Malmesbury war workers recognize themselves and are prompted to write their own version of the past. Mass-Observation was primarily concerned with offering a service to management; the interests of the women themselves were secondary to the interests of the war machine which is presumably why the women were not invited at the time to comment on the study whereas Mr Lipman and his colleagues were able to comment copiously. All the same, *War Factory* is a fascinating book and this edition gives us another chance to re-evaluate its contribution to our understanding of the quality and constraints to our mothers' and grandmothers' lives.

Dorothy Sheridan
Archivist
Mass-Observation Archive
University of Sussex
1987

INDUSTRIAL SURVEY

by

TOM HARRISSON
(*Director of Mass-Observation*)

"I found the poems in the fields,
And only wrote them down . . ."
JOHN CLARE

As A SOCIAL research organisation, Mass-Observation has necessarily concerned itself with the great changes in industry, industrial personnel and labour relations during the war. From the long-term point of view, physical, psychological, social and economic changes inside our factories are profoundly important as well as interesting. We have already published one detailed report on certain aspects of this problem.[1] This study attracted the interest of industrialists, and gave a still wider field of contact. Some invited us to investigate specific problems. One of these was a famous firm which now specialises in a vital all-Services product. On the basis of "People in Production" I was asked to examine the set-up in their new key factory, small but crucial.

SET-UP

After superficial examination of difficulties which were slowing production, I suggested closer analysis might interest us and prove useful to them. This volume is one result, from our point of view. From the firm's point of view, analysis did reveal many points which have led to improvements. The Works Manager pays his polite tribute (page 125); he also describes the background from his point of view, thus:

"On the outbreak of War it was originally intended that the Production Unit should consist of not more than 150–200 persons. War developments, however, necessitated a far greater output than was originally intended, and successive increases have, during a period of two and a half years,

[1] "People in Production" No. 3 of the Advertising Service Guild's Bulletin *Change*. Further editions have since been published by Messrs. John Murray, and in an abbreviated version as a Penguin Special.

put the total to well over four times that figure. The original location was chosen with a view to a maximum of say 250 employees, which would match with a geographical environment having a population of 3,500 to 4,000 within a five-mile radius. The actual increase in personnel has meant that the number employed is disproportionate to the size of the local population, and the necessity of drafting in employees from outside, consequent transport, billeting, and other problems, have provided the main difficulties with which the Management has been faced.

"The Winter of 1941–42 saw saturation point reached in personnel, and the problems of War fatigue, lack of concentration, and general absence of 'morale' reached proportions which made it necessary to have some objective survey undertaken, with a view to taking into account the 'Worm's eye view'. It is notorious that a Factory Manager is at the apex of a triangle; in spite of close personal observation what happens down below is not easily apparent, and the channels of communication in both directions are in most cases through parties not exactly disinterested, but with views on Labour and Management questions which may differ widely from the Management itself.

"In calling in Mass-Observation to perform this task of observation and short-circuiting normal channels through which information filters, it was realised that it was akin to taking a decision to be psycho-analysed, not for the purpose of finding out the pleasant things about oneself, but the unpleasant factors which are either conscious but deliberately ignored, or sub-conscious and therefore unknown. Management problems tend to fall very much into both these categories, and it must be added that the Management in question was prepared for some rude shocks and certainly received them."

METHOD: QUANTITATIVE OR QUALITATIVE?

The greater part of this investigation was undertaken by a highly trained and experienced Cambridge graduate, married, one child; she has worked with Mass-Observation for the past four years. Generally, Mass-Observation employs a team of trained objective investigators working simultaneously, checking this with information of a subjective nature from some of the persons actually being observed.[1] In the present case,

[1] For critical accounts of Mass-Observation method, readers may consult recent papers in *The Reprints of the Manchester Statistical Society* (April 1943) by J. Ferraby; *Agenda* (Aug. 1943), by Celia Goller; *British Journal of Medical Psychology* (April 1942), by Dr. P. E. Vernon; and the *American Journal of Sociology* (January 1943) by H. D. Willcock.

largely owing to the small size of the unit and the difficult problems of "security" involved, it was decided after experiment that the main study should be made by one investigator moving about within the framework of the problem.

Many of the phenomena which face the sociologist *are not* initially amenable to quantitative study until qualitative evaluation has been achieved. There is a strong tendency to regard only the numerical description of humans as scientific. This largely derives from two sources. First, most of our "social scientists" have not trained in scientific method, but in literary, philosophic, historical and other methods. This causes a feeling of inferiority, of self-questioning about personal scientificness. Statistics provide one compensation, a symbol of rectitude. Second, objective study of ourselves is so psychologically trying, so against the grain of personal prejudice, that there is an unconscious tendency to avoid the full implications of an unbiased sociology. Here again, the consolation of statistics provides an "escape". It is easy to believe that by asking a "random sample" of two thousand people what they think about the Prime Minister, you have achieved something socially scientific. Actually, at best you have found out what they say to a stranger in the street, which may differ widely from what they *think*. Ask the whole population the same question, your sample figures will not be altered by more than 4 per cent. Therefore you can conclude the results are "scientifically accurate". They are mathematically accurate, but humanly they may be no more than reportage of unanalysed, even misunderstood, public *words* of the moment. One does not detect methodological error merely by magnifying the method.

Social Science has been backward. It is important for civilisation that it should soon mature. It is therefore important that social scientists should be perfectly clear about what they are doing, and how. The *anthropological* method, freely applied to black people, can be as illuminating among white. It has still scarcely begun to be applied here at home. Confucius was right: "Truth must not depart from human nature. If what is regarded as truth departs from human nature, it may not be regarded as truth." The qualitative approach is used daily by biologists, surgeons, geologists. No-one doubts that in such hands the results are "scientific". The statistical obsession among sociologists obscures the parallel. Thus Professor A. M. Carr-Saunders, brilliant head of the London School of Economics, concluded a recent important B.B.C. series of talks entitled "Man Observes Himself":

> "There is one thing that troubles me about all this. Measuring, counting, calculating chances is very useful nowadays; it's really more than that; we cannot do without it. If all the present talk of planning is to lead to anything, we must do a great deal of measuring beforehand; otherwise the plans will not produce the results we expect from them. Now people don't mind answering questions about themselves and their affairs if they are sure that the questions are necessary and that something useful will come of it. But people would not like it if they had reason to think that the questions were useless and that they were being bothered to no purpose."

The one thing that bothers Professor Carr-Saunders is not that statistical methods may be inadequate, but that citizens may tire of them. He nowhere proposes applying even statistical method to normal *behaviour*, for instance conversation (about which we have virtually no information). He considers *only* the statistical questionnaire, the stranger interview. For many lesser social-scientists, question and answer, tabulated by Hollerith, have become the main aim. As William Blake asked: "What kind of Intellects must he have who sees only the Colours of Things and not the Form of Things?" Uncontrolled accumulation of figures may actually obscure the HUMAN problem. To mention only one example, no social subject has been more statistically studied than the birth-rate. Yet the *Times* correctly said (June 12th) that there is "a startling lack of factual knowledge". The qualitative study of the trajectory from conception to birth has barely been attempted. In such matters *solely* quantitative methods tend to endless pursuit of the WHAT, while neglecting the vital WHY. A synthesis of both approaches is long overdue all through the sociological field.

RESULTS: TYPICALITY? APATHY!

It will be clear that this limited, qualitative study is not supposed to be "typical" of anything. Those who are concerned to relate it to a wider background might consult the "People in Production" report. We were called in to make the present investigation precisely because there were peculiarities and abnormalities in the unit (cf. page 18). Nevertheless the results suggest certain mental conditions among a number of female workers, mainly young, which are so striking that they cannot lightly be dismissed as "peculiar". The results are in line with other recent work,—for example on political apathy, passive leisure, youth morality. Underlying the life of young working women to-day there is a background of aimlessness, irresponsibility and boredom (cf. page 113). Beneath the justified propaganda about war workers, other and more lasting factors have to be recognised and considered for the future. Some of the present study makes depressing reading. Now the war is going much better, we can afford to be more open about ourselves. In this factory we see how industrial morale can go under certain circumstances (e.g. page 30). This is not industrial morale at its lowest, for here the disturbing factors were often removable owing to a sympathetic management. Yet the management (see below) do not suggest that our main picture is overdrawn. Indeed they were more depressed about their workpeople before the survey than after reading this report.

Taken in conjunction with the other fieldwork, these factory girls emphasise *the dangerous decline in positive citizenship*, especially among the young. This decline subtly threatens the health of all democracy. It has the germs of a general decline in the essential sense of civilised humanity. But although Molly, Edith, Peggy, Hilda, Sadie (of Chapter 4) may be variously adrift, their hearts still beat in the right place, of this I have no doubt. Wherever we turn to-day we find evidence of this cultural passivity. The *laissez faire* of leisure, and its dangerous separation from work, is immediately and primarily responsible. There is nothing here which cannot be overcome by resolute remedy. Yet few diseases have been less diagnosed. Even now, when Britain is a-hum with plans, these basic social and "spiritual" matters are practically ignored.

FACTORY LIFE IN PRINT

Considering the vast part industry plays in Britain, there are remarkably few modern books about daily factory *life*. Even industrial *novels* are quite rare. This has indeed been true over a century. Since the war thousands of writers have told of evacuees in the village, heroes in the blitz, airmen and sailors, girls in Government Departments. There is hardly anything worth reading on fitter and foreman, conscript girl, volunteer housewife, labourer. Inez Holden's novel, *Night Shift*, has some genuine feelings; J. B. Priestley's *Daylight on Saturday*, a very understanding tale of an aircraft factory, incidentally reflecting some of the confused ethics of American James Burnham's *The Managerial Revolution*; and Mark Benney's frankly propagandist but informed *Over to Bombers*. On the scientific side, statistical studies made by the Industrial Health Research Board and other bodies[1]; but practically nothing about *social* and *mental* processes within contemporary industry.

The able Austrian social psychologist, Dr. Marie Jahoda, is one of the few to make a recent examination of normal patterns among a group of factory girls.[2] She must have been handicapped by imperfect command of working class language and labyrinth; she deserves the more credit for trying to break new ground. As she says:

> ". . . the workers were not [at first] informed, in order to keep the situation as unaffected as possible by the observer. After the first month it became advisable to explain the research project . . ."

Alas, such revelations are a regular feature of sociological attempts at penetration, for highly educated people can seldom sustain the appearance of anonymity. The ability to appear and remain average is the acid test of an investigator's understanding of his or her human material. Compare the present study; *no one* in the factory, apart from two managers, had any idea they were being studied. That was the essence of the affair. How *can* factory girls behave "naturally" with a visiting "psychologist" visibly analysing them?

Yet Miss Jahoda does not hesitate to generalise her "several months" study: "the problems presented here are assumed to be universal in factory life, although they may be tackled and solved in different ways elsewhere." This ambitious if ambiguous statement is *not* substantiated by concrete information. Instead she makes a series of subjective statements, like this initial one:

> "A factory is no logical construction but a social reality. The variety of social relations in it can therefore not be reduced to a simple scheme. The concatenation of various elements in a group situation is a social factor in itself which must not be neglected lest one fails to produce the right picture. Thus, though applying the terminology introduced above, an analysis of the socio-psychological problem of the group situation cannot be restricted to the notions implied by 'horizontal' and 'vertical' contact."

[1] These are fully discussed in "People in Production".

[2] "Some Socio-Psychological Problems of Factory Life," by M. Jahoda; *British Journal of Psychology*, XXXI, pp. 191–206.

Such imposing vocabulary might carry the weight if supported by correspondingly elaborate *evidence*. The first sentence, read once, hurriedly, might sound like learned sociology. Read again, carefully, it boils away. It is easy to recede into such tautological grandiloquence when faced with ordinary people living normal lives in ordinary environments. Jahoda's paper is full of parallel instances, which when examined fall short on the elementary scientific criteria of clarity, precision, objectivity, and evidence. She draws three characteristically broad conclusions; the first will illustrate:

> "The social relationship in the horizontal dimension is 'equalitarian'; the vertical relationship between workers and foremen and head-girls is 'dictatorial'; the vertical relationship between the workers and the management is 'patriarchal', and also ambivalent."

Few factories would really tolerate such a relationship, few foremen dare dictatorial methods. The situation described in Chapter 7 below, is nearer the mark. There are other indications that Jahoda had misunderstood her own study situation. Be that as it may, her interesting paper contains many unsupported generalities, stressed here to indicate the crudity of most attempts, so far, to examine daily patterns qualitatively, humanly, socially. We have to face this amateur attitude in serious, youthful sociology. Mass-Observation suffers seriously from it, too. . . .

FOUR QUALIFICATIONS

This book stands almost exactly as originally drafted in report form for the client. Four exceptions must be noted:

(i) On security grounds, anything relating to the firm's fascinating production process is omitted.

(ii) On personal grounds, identifications are obscured.

(iii) For reasons of space, some technical, economic or detailed passages are omitted.

(iv) We asked the management to criticise and correct. The Works and Labour Manager's remarks are printed as written on the MSS., and without comment. They give a view not directly studied in the survey. Like all social evidence, where their words contradict others, no single one can be said to be exactly in the right or wrong. All attitudes are relevant, however prejudiced or informed.

TOM HARRISSON.

In the Army,
September, 1943.

SECTION I

BACKGROUND

I

THE TOWN AND THE NEWCOMERS

IN A TINY country town of ancient cottages and winding street, with traditions going back to Saxon times, there has suddenly sprung up in a matter of months, a modern war factory employing nearly 1,000 people, staffed mainly by brisk, town-bred men who have no connection with the locality.

And as if this shock was not enough by itself, it came almost simultaneously with the wartime invasion of evacuees, ministry officials, soldiers, etc., etc., that has been the lot of most country towns. No wonder that the local population has barely yet woken from the state of dazed bewilderment into which it was stunned by this avalanche of events. Their peaceful old-world town is gone; and in its place is something resembling a London railway terminus, with its endless comings and goings of strangers from all parts of the country; with its atmosphere of irritable bustle, impersonal pushing and hurrying.[1]

But this invasion of strangers was not only bewildering. It was also annoying, and highly inconvenient. In peacetime the overcrowding of local buses and shops, the impossibility of getting into the cinema on Saturday afternoons, would probably have been forgiven for the sake of all the extra money that was being brought into the town. But now there is no such consolation. Shopkeepers no longer have any desire to attract new customers; a new customer is a nuisance rather than an asset—an unwanted drain on his dwindling supplies. And while housewives might be pleased enough to put themselves out to accommodate holiday makers at a high price, it is a different matter to have the house crowded and all the extra housework for 25/- a week, out of which two good meals and all lighting, heating, home, have to be provided. To the ordinary country housewife, who reads the paper rarely and only has the vaguest ideas about what is going on outside her own town, these people

[1] The proportion of imported employees to original inhabitants over a 5 mile radius is approximately 30%—(*Labour Manager*).

come not as an essential and inevitable part of the common war effort, but quite meaninglessly out of the blue; like a swarm of locusts they arrive without warning and without reasons, to eat up the already scarce food supplies; to buy up all the favourite brands of soap and patent medicines; to consume all the fish in the fish and chip shops, leaving her only chips; to cram the local cinema at weekends so that she and her husband can't get near it.

And to crown all, these newcomers usually arrive in a bad temper. Only a small number of them come here because they *want* to; a big majority dislike the idea of coming, and are prepared to dislike anything and everything about the place;[1] they are continually comparing it unfavourably with their own homes. Here is a typical conversation between two newly-arrived C-class men from Bristol (it did not take place actually in the hearing of their landlady, but she could not mistake their general mood):

"My God, what a dump! Oh, my *God* what a dump!"

"Do you think you'll have to stay here long?"

"God knows. When they send you somewhere quite bloody they usually try to keep you there."

"I wonder what the pubs are like?"

"I don't wonder, I can guess. Beer watered down so it tastes like dishwater, and all sold out by eight o'clock."

"Hm. What the devil will we do in the evenings?"

"Go to bed, I suppose. I expect Mrs. Whats-it here will ration the light to us, or something, so we can't read. They're always out to do you down in these places."

"I don't think I shall be here more than a few weeks. I think I shall be able to get my release after that."

"Wish *I* could. When I came for my interview I tried to make myself as dumb as was humanly possible without being certified, but it wasn't any good. I got a letter telling me to come on Monday morning. I got there at two o'clock instead of in the morning, and that night they put me in a place that was the next best thing to a workhouse. I didn't sleep in the bed at all, I had to sit up in a chair. I couldn't put my head on that pillow. So this morning I went in and told them they

[1] This has only been the case since compulsory labour regulations for both male and female employees. Previously, especially during the blitz period, people flooded into the district from blitzed areas being desirous of working in a quiet country town, but as the unpleasant memories of bombing faded, the evacuees tended to become as restless as compulsorily transferred persons.—(*Works Manager*).

could either find me another billet, or they could pay my bill at a hotel, or I would take the first bus back home.

"The result is this! *This* is where I'm to live, apparently—or rather exist!

"Oh well. I suppose I'll go out and get pickled."[1]

This sort of superficial attitude of discontent and grumbling infuriates the locals. They take it as an insult to themselves and their town, an exhibition of snobbishness and superiority. And in part it is; but a much greater part is merely the expression of a bewilderment and sense of upheaval quite as great as the local people's own.

Not realising this, and not fully realising either that these people have been *forced* to come here by or events outside authority, the locals, take a very firm line about this grumbling. Again and again one hears remarks like:

1. "If she don't like it here, why don't she go back where she came from? *We* wouldn't miss her."
2. "If we're not good enough for him, then let him take himself off and find somewhere where he *is* satisfied."
3. "They just come down here to get work, and then when they've got it it's just grumble, grumble all the time. If they don't like it, then what they come for? That's what I always say."

This kind of hostility is directed more against the factory and its employees than against the other newcomers, because the factory is the least understood kind of activity in a place like this. Soldiers are accepted; everyone realises that soldiers are dumped down suddenly in strange places and for no apparent reason. The townspeople are willing to tolerate any inconvenience that they may cause. The Air Ministry, too, because of its title, is allowed to have an unquestionable (even if undiscoverable) importance. But the factory is a mere excrescence. While it might have been welcomed before the war as providing new opportunities for employment, there is no advantage in this now, for everyone who wants to be is already fully employed. Its importance to the war is only vaguely realised, though, in view of the low level of war interest here, it is doubtful whether

[1] This is an example of the kind of exaggeration which it is "the thing" to put over to newcomers. It gives the older hand a sense of superiority to give the "low down" to new arrivals. It is very commonplace in the army with reference to the officers.

it would make much difference to their attitude if they *did* realise reasons for its existence (particularly for its existence here). It is a puzzle to most, who are very ready to dislike its employees. To start with, there is the feeling that one always gets in a non-industrial area; that factory workers are a very low class of people; that the girls are "not nice"; that it is a low sort of occupation altogether.

Some of them, too, regard it as a soft sort of job, and there is a lot of talk about men going there to dodge the army:

> "They ought to be shot, some of those fellows up there. They've got nothing to do, and they're just sitting tight there because they're frightened they'll have to join the army." (M35C)
>
> "There's a lot of men jumped in there at the beginning of the war hoping to be reserved. I'd like to see a good comb-out up there, to catch out those sort of people." (M50C)
>
> "There isn't anything that a woman couldn't do just as well. It makes me sick to see these great lumps of men hiding away up there while our boys do the fighting. The cowardly swine!" (F40D)[1]

They are accused of having no work to do—there was a joke going round the town at one time that goes as follows:

> "A man up at E was fined to-day."
> "What for?" asks the hearer.
> "He was caught working!"

There is a lot of gossip on these lines, mostly about the various members of the staff:

> "They've got a nice job for themselves, those two (members of the staff). Mrs. H. is supposed to be working in the factory, but *I've* seen her wandering about the streets at eleven in the morning. She's the dodger type; I wouldn't trust that woman further than I could throw a bull by the tail.[2] And

[1] These are excellent examples of the kind of ill-founded criticism so ably analysed in *People in Production*. The less knowledge the more exaggerated the statements. Recently, a local Councillor, who could have had any information he liked to ask for, actually stated in public that the factory was working part-time, whereas it is in fact working in excess of the minimum laid down by the Ministry of Labour. Added to this ill-founded criticism is the general attitude of "He's different, let's heave a brick at him."—(*Works Manager*).

[2] Actually the employee concerned was the Factory Billeting Officer—(*Works Manager*).

that Mr. G.; why isn't he in the army? Anyway, he's no good for a job like that. He's got a very uneducated voice. You'd have expected a man of culture in his postion."[1] (M40C)

But underlying all these incidental bickerings and jealousies is the basic distrust of the countryman for strangers from the town. And in this case they are not isolated innocuous strangers, anxious to win the goodwill of the local people and find a place for themselves in the social life of the community. They are unwilling and disgruntled strangers, anxious only to get out of the place as soon as they know how, and go back to their own communities. Such strangers jar on people who have had their town to themselves for a thousand years.[2]

2

THE FACTORY. FIRST IMPRESSIONS

THIS, THEN, IS the setting of the factory. Its rapid growth has taken place in the midst of a rural community that is fast disintegrating under the impact of new and ever changing conditions. And this same atmosphere of instability and bewilderment is as characteristic of the factory as it is of the town. Very few indeed of the workers (or indeed of the staff) have had any real experience of industrial life. Most of the unskilled female workers (and it is with these that this investigation will be mainly concerned) are country girls recruited either from

[1] Actually a University graduate and ex-Assistant Head of an important secondary school (but his dialect is not local)—(*Works Manager*).

[2] This tends to be an over-simplification. Longer residence in the area would have shown Mass-Observation that for a town of its size the lack of social life is phenomenal. The Vicar rarely calls; there is no Sewing Circle; no Trade Union, political or other Club, with the exception of a dull Y.M.C.A. handed over to the Military since War broke out. There is nowhere discernible a nucleus of inhabitants, new or old, who co-operate for any purpose whatever. Even the shopkeepers refuse to form a Chamber of Commerce or Wartime Traders' Committee. If there had been some such nucleus on which to build, the problems which have arisen would have been solved much more easily. Unfortunately, among the class of person who usually does "public work", the loss of domestic servants, at first voluntarily, and later by conscription to the factory, has been a factor which has very definitely set a large number of the middle class against the industrial intrusion.

The fact that they are now engaged on important War work instead of attending to private needs is completely ignored, and as in very many other instances the view taken is purely subjective—(*Works Manager*).

the town itself or from outlying villages, and factory life is something quite new to them. For this reason, the following chapters must not be regarded as describing a typical *industrial* life at all; for there are none of the industrial traditions and background with which the true industrial worker is surrounded. Rather it is a study of rural adaptation (and failure of adaptation) to a new and startling industrial situation suddenly forced upon them. For the factory has no roots in the place: it has no history of natural growth and development. It was simply dropped there, like a bomb; and just as in the case of a bomb, everyone concerned had to adapt themselves to the situation as best they could. It is with this process that the following chapters will mainly be concerned.[1]

The actual site of the factory is what was, two years ago, a large country house, set in lovely grounds about half a mile outside the town. And in spite of the sound of machinery, the camouflage netting, and the mess of new buildings, something of the house's original charm remains. Here and there amid the ordinary drabness and ugliness of a factory interior are sudden flashes from the past; a lovely polished oak staircase leads up to the offices; every here and there old beams and latticed windows strike a pleasantly incongruous note. And outside, although most of the grounds have been scarred and spoilt by new buildings, both completed and in the process of construction, there are still some pleasant features left. A curving drive arched over with trees forms the entrance, and just in front of the main building is a stretch of water surrounded by shrubs and bushes, and still inhabited by a family of ducks.

The first impressions of the newcomer are therefore not unpleasant. And in addition to the fact that the surroundings are really much less forbidding than most people expect when they learn that they are to work in a large factory,[2] the authori-

[1] This paragraph is very important. The absence of *any* industrial background at home is a factor which cannot be exaggerated. The tradition of the factory whistle or "knocker up" or any other familiar part of the industrial background acquaints all members of a family with the necessity for starting and finishing work at a given time. This is an essential part of any factory discipline (for want of a better word). For a large percentage of the employees drafted in locally, their work at the factory was their first experience of having to work to a strict timetable, and that is why the absence of any industrial background referred to above is of such importance—(*Works Manager*).

[2] This is quite true. Most of the inhabitants in this rural area previously could only think of factories in terms of belching chimneys and clattering machines. The absence of any such outward signs of industrial activity actually

ties really do seem to take considerable trouble to make a new employee arriving from a distance feel welcome. She is taken in the car to a billet that has already been found for her, and then is taken up to the factory for her interview and formal application.

All the new girls I met seemed to have found this interview a much less formidable affair than they had expected, and were rather pleasantly surprised by it. Of the Labour Manager, they say in surprised tones: "Wasn't he nice!" and almost their only complaint is about the number of forms they had to fill in:

> "I thought I'd never get to the end of it! As soon as I'd written in one, they'd give me another!" (F20C)
>
> "I was in there for an hour, all that palaverment with the registrations." (F25D).
>
> "They ask you every bloody thing, bar what lipstick do you use?" (F30D)

But the horror of these forms is very much mitigated by the friendly and informal attitude which the office girls adopt. There is none of the brusqueness and preoccupied haste which is so characteristic of Labour Exchange girls. On the contrary, they are as helpful and sympathetic as they can be, helping over the difficult parts and reassuring about the doubtful and unanswerable ones. An investigator's report on her own experiences in this office illustrates the atmosphere.

"I was shown into a small office at the top of a flight of stone steps. It was light and cheerful, with a number of latticed windows, and a low ceiling; probably it was a spare bedroom in the old days. It contained two long deal tables, a desk, and a number of shelves. Four girls were working there, when I came in, two of them at typewriters, and a middle-aged foreman was leaning against the radiator, chatting with the girls. The whole atmosphere was informal and friendly, and also rather disorganised. The girls are continually asking each other who has put what where:

> 'Where's the absentee list for Thursday?'
> 'In the file, isn't it?'
> 'Which one? The absentee file?'
> 'Yes—a flat one. Isn't it there?'
> 'Well—I don't know . . .'

---

caused such comments as "It can't be a factory, they have no chimney", or "How can there be a factory in what was a country house?"—(*Works Manager*).

"Both start to hunt about on different parts of the table. Suddenly a loudspeaker in the corner of the room blares out:

'Stand by for an announcement. Stop all machines. The Home Guard parade on Sunday morning will take place to-morrow at ten a.m.'

'I'll be in bed, sister,' remarks the foreman. The girls laugh.

'It's a job getting up these mornings, isn't it?' says one of them.

'Wicked. Ought to be stopped!' says the foreman.

'It's all right for you men, when *you* finish, all you've got to do is to go home, and your warm boots are put under your nose, and your supper is put under your nose, and all you have to do is to sit yourself down and eat it. But us married women, we have to get the supper and warm the boots when *we* get home from work!'

'You can't put that one over to *me*! I'm a married man myself!'

"Well. Isn't that what happens when you get home from work?"

'Cor blimey!' is all he says.

"Meanwhile, one of the girls had given me various forms to fill in. She explained exactly what had to be filled in and what hadn't, and then hovered about, ready to answer questions. Whenever I didn't know the answer to a question (e.g. names and exact dates of all places of employment since leaving school) she consoled me by saying gaily that it didn't matter; nobody ever got it right.[1]

"Occasionally as I worked at this the loudspeaker would blare startlingly from the corner:

'Calling Mr. Jones!' or 'Calling Mr. Smith!'

"Apparently the idea of this phenomenon is that when there are telephone calls for some member of the staff who isn't in his office, this microphone announcing it to every room and department ensures that he is bound to hear it, and won't have to be hunted for all over the factory. When I first heard it I found it most startling and disconcerting, but one soon gets

[1] It should be pointed out here that the Observer was known only to the Labour Manager in order to avoid the possibility of any misconceived idea of a "spy" being present, or alternatively of special treatment being afforded by Foreman, etc. The Manager was particularly careful not to contact the Observer until the end of the period, so as to avoid any possibility of influencing opinion either way by personal impression—(*Works Manager*).

used to it, and it is no more than a very faint irritation. Indeed, when on very monotonous work, it is almost a relief sometimes; it allows one's mind, which has probably come to the end of all available topics for thought, to drift idly off into a new track: 'Oh, so he's got a telephone call; I wonder what it's about?' But in other circumstances very mild annoyance is the usual reaction, as shown by frequent murmured comments:

> 'Shut up, you twerp!'
> 'Oh, calling your grandmother!'
> 'Cut it out!'

"The office where I was filling in the forms served as an ante-room to the Labour Manager's own office, which is separated from it by a wooden partition containing a large pane of glass, through which he can see everything going on in the outer office. The Labour Manager himself is constantly going in and out, but this does not stop the chatter and gossip among the office girls at all. They seem to be on good terms with him, and there is no 'S-sh! Here he comes!' about it.

"When I had filled in all the forms, one of the girls took me down to see the machine shop, where I was going to work. My impressions of it at this first sight were very blurred; just a lot of machines in a largish building, and a good deal of noise that made it difficult to talk in ordinary tones. My escort made no attempt to put over a line about its attractions. She said candidly:

> 'This is the worst shop, really. I would hate to work here, but I think some of them like it. It's a good thing somebody does! You hear them singing sometimes when you go past.'

"On the following morning, Monday, I was able to form my own estimate of the machine shop. But whatever fate is in store for one, it is certainly very pleasant to have the unterrifying introduction to the factory that has just been described. It also makes one slightly more likely to get on well with the life in general. For, as pointed out in the last chapter, most new employees tend to arrive in a pretty disgruntled frame of mind, and anything which can be done to soften this mood before they reach their billets is all to the good.[1] For the final relations

[1] This points to a development of our system of interviewing and consequent first impressions. I feel that at least an hour or so should be spent on each new employee showing a rough idea of the factory layout and where their particular job will fit into the general scheme of things—(*Labour Manager*).

between landlady and billetee depend a lot on the impression created on the first evening.

"A final rather pleasant touch to the first day's interview is to find that the porter recognises one going out at the gate. 'Get you fixed up all right?' he said as I passed. Obviously it is part of his job to recognise newcomers after one sight of them, but it also gives the new employee a feeling of being welcome as an individual, not just a cipher in the machine."

SECTION II

INSIDE THE FACTORY

3

A DAY IN THE MACHINE SHOP

THE MACHINE SHOP stands by itself a little away from the main building. It occupies what was formerly the stables, and in spite of the clocking-in cards at the entrance and the hum of machinery within, it still gives much more the impression of a stable than of a factory, with its rough walls, high windows, and dark cobwebby corners. The main part of the room is occupied by half a dozen benches, on which are mounted a number of small machines of various kinds. At the back are a few larger machines standing by themselves, and all round the walls are entrances into store rooms, rooms for special electrical work, and so on. Altogether, about a hundred women are employed there, and a score or so of men.

At eight a.m. the factory buzzer sounds, and a wild scramble starts at the entrance of the machine shop (an ordinary wooden small door, such as might lead into any private room). The night workers are trying to clock out exactly the same moment as the day workers are clocking in; only one person can clock in or out at the same time, and as there is no system of queueing, or order of any kind, it is a case of all-against-all, in which the strongest or heaviest wins.[1] Everyone is in a hurry—the day workers because only three minutes' grace is allowed for clocking in after the buzzer goes, the night workers simply because this is the moment they have been awaiting for the last twelve hours or so. The scrimmage, though ruthless, is fairly good-humoured, and a good deal of joking goes on among the groans and exclamations:

> "Oh, my lord, my handbag's come open again. Thought I'd lost it that time. OH, my lord, they'll be having the arms off of me before they're through!"

[1] Machine Shop clocking. It certainly does not appear to be as good as it might be, though it has been improved and the addition of an extra clock now available will clear this—(*Labour Manager*).

"Come on, sister. Give him a shove! You won't get nowhere here without you shove for it!"

"Oh, my foot!"

"You shouldn't leave it on the floor, then it wouldn't get trod on." (*General laugh from immediate neighbourhood.*)

"O-ooh! This'll be the finish of me!"

Through it all, the voice of the doorkeeper can be heard occasionally, appealing plaintively to the night workers:

"Let the young ladies clock in; stand back please and let the day workers clock in."

After getting through this, there is a secondary scramble in the cloakroom, which is small for the number of people using it. The congestion would be even worse were it not for the fact that a number of girls hang about at the benches with their coats and scarves on, waiting for the crush to subside before they go in.[1] There is no sense of hurry in the cloakroom at this hour (there are no definite penalties attached to being late on the bench, once one has actually clocked in to the building), and a lot of people take a quarter of an hour or more changing from coats into overalls; a great deal of talk and chatter goes on. Just for illustration, a verbatim record was made of the talk one Tuesday morning the middle of February (a day chosen at random, for no reason other than its similarity to all the other days):

"Who's got my overall?" says a sulky, dark-haired girl, pushing about among the chaos of coats and overalls hanging up. "This is my peg, I left it hanging there last night. Who's got it?"

"You're the mug, leaving anything in this dump. They'll pinch anything here. Pinch the milk out of your tea if you don't watch it."

"I lost a lovely pair of gloves here last winter. Real fur they were. I wasn't half wild. I only put them down a minute, while I went for my bag."

[1] Unfortunately only too true. The very rapid expansion necessitating the utilisation of every bit of available space for machinery has seriously reduced the amount of cloakroom space, and it is only now that we are in a position to provide extra accommodation. Even in sections of the Works that are very well provided with cloakrooms, however, the same reluctance to start work in the morning is to be observed—(*Works Manager*).

"Awful, isn't it, come to think of it. You can't put anything down."

"Where's Edie this morning?"

"She wasn't on the bus, because he waited for her. At the corner. Don't know what's happened to her."

"Perhaps she went to the dance last night and didn't wake up."

"No, she didn't go to the dance, because Peggy was there, and she says she never saw her."

"I thought she was going. She said she was going."

"She said she would if Lil did, but I don't think Lil did go. She said she wasn't feeling like it, she didn't think she would, not getting home so late."

"You can't go anywhere, can you; by the time you've had a wash and had your supper it's time for bed, isn't it?"

"That's right. It's wicked."

"Well, all I know is, I wish it was eight o'clock now."

"Oh, wouldn't it be lovely! If we was all dressing to go home now, and the buzzer just sounding!"

"I wish it was Saturday."

"It's wishing our lives away, that's all we do here," says a sad-looking woman of about forty, with ginger hair growing grey. "When I was in London, the time couldn't go slow enough for me. All the things I had to do, and now it's just wish, wish, wish. I wish it was all over, that's my wish. I'm about fed up with it."

"O-ooh! Mind where you're going!"—as a new surge of arrivals sets everyone staggering once more.

"My stocking's gone again. I felt it go as I got on the bus. That's the third pair of stockings this week."

"Awful, isn't it, with the coupons."

"Look at my lunch!" A tall, fair-haired girl with heavily lipsticked mouth holds up, with shouts of laughter, a sodden parcel of sandwiches, soaked by the rain.

"Look at Lil's lunch! You'd better eat them right away, Lil. They'll all come to pieces."

"Blimey, is that your lunch, Lil?"

"Bit wet, aren't they Lil?"

"What are you going to do with them?"

"I'm going to eat 'em," says Lil doggedly. "But I'm not going to eat 'em now. They'll dry off."

"Good thing she's not fussy," says one of the girls, as Lil edges her way through the crowd. "I wouldn't eat them, would you? Not like that!"

At a quarter-past eight there are still only about half the girls actually working at their machines (the official time for starting work is at eight o'clock when the buzzer goes). Not till half-past is there anything approaching the whole lot working.[1] There is a marked tendency every morning for the older women to start work sooner than the young ones; the half-dozen or so women of over forty who work in this shop are almost always at their machines before five-past eight[2]—a time when few of the other machines are in action.

There are various types of machine in the shop—drilling, tapping, etc., each of them operated by one girl, sitting down. On almost all of them the work is very simple and monotonous, involving simply placing the part in position (it is usually impossible to do this wrong) and then the raising or lowering of a handle, or some such action. Usually one can work at one's own speed, letting the finished parts pile up on the bench or in a cardboard box, until someone comes and takes them away; there is little feeling of hurry, or having one's pace dictated by the machine itself, as in continuous belt work. With a few exceptions, the work here involved neither mental nor physical effort of any kind. It is, in fact, just the type of work one hears educated people at war work exhibitions speak of with horror: "I'd go crazy, doing that all day." "The monotony would kill me," and so on. As the observer puts it: "I was particularly interested to find out what it *does* feel like to be employed thus for hours at a stretch. To my surprise, I found that the boredom is far less than people imagine. In fact, for at any rate the first couple of hours, the work is definitely pleasant, rather like knitting in a fairly plain pattern. After the rush and scramble of getting up and coming to work through the sleet of a February morning, hurrying to get there in time, fighting to clock in at the door, it is restful and pleasant to sit down in a warm room, with nothing to do but fiddle with little bits of metal, and to know that for twelve hours one will not have to think or worry about anything at all."

This feeling is naturally stronger in a newcomer, but undoubtedly throughout the room there is an atmosphere of greater concentration on the job during the first hours of the morning than at any other time in the day. The amount of

[1] Foremen should definitely be instructed to take stronger action, with a view to pointing out the serious waste of time involved. (See Appendix.)—(*Labour Manager*).

[2] The older women employed are almost exclusively evacuees from industrial towns with previous industrial experience—(*Works Manager*).

talking and idling is small, and there is little of the "clock watching" which forms one of the main features of the latter half of the day.

The first break is at ten o'clock, for ten minutes. About half the people go up to the canteen for cheese rolls and cups of tea, the rest stay around the shop, knitting, eating sandwiches and talking. After that work continues till dinner time at one o'clock.[1]

It is at a little before eleven that the first signs of slacking off begin to appear. People start going out to the cloakroom and hanging about there for long periods, doing their hair, talking, eating the cakes and sandwiches they have brought for dinner and tea. The subject of what time it is (which by four in the afternoon, as we shall see, has become almost an obsession) begins to appear in conversations:

"It's five past eleven."

"That clock's gone slow again. It's nearly ten past. Jack, don't you make it nearly ten past?"

"Eh?"

"It's ten past eleven, isn't it? Isn't that clock slow?"

"That's not slow. That's right."

"What, is it only five past?"

"That's right."

"Oh!" Groans from both girls. "Only five past!"

The official time for dinner is one o'clock, and the official time for getting ready for it is five minutes to; actually preparations start a long while before that. Between half-past twelve and five to one the cloakrooms are locked (the idea of this is to prevent people getting ready before the appointed time), but what happens as a result of this is that from twelve-twenty a crowd of girls is to be found in the cloakroom washing their hands, preparatory to going back to the bench and doing nothing whatever for half an hour, so as not to get their hands dirty again before dinner. Another dodge for getting ready before time is the bucket of water in the welding room. It is filled from the water hose there, and the girls who work in that part of the room, and their friends, always wash their hands there before time.

[1] An interesting point here is that the workers in this section have recently *asked* to have their morning break in the Shop itself, and they now have their tea and rolls brought down to them. This would seem to argue against the view that getting away from the Shop into the Canteen is a "looked forward to occasion"—(*Labour Manager*).

The real reason for all this ingenuity being expended on circumventing an apparently reasonable rule is that there are only three basins in the cloakroom[1] and it is quite impossible for everyone to wash their black and oily hands in the five minutes allowed for it. If the rules were kept, it would mean that a lot of people would not get up to the canteen till a quarter past one or later; and the loss of even *one* minute of any of the breaks is regarded as a tragedy. The anxiety not to miss a single second is always marked at dinner time. At a minute or so before one, people stand by the door poised like athletes for a race, waiting to rush at the first note of the buzzer. A certain amount of this anxiety is because being late means being at the end of the queue in the canteen; but it is certainly not all due to this, because people who bring their own sandwiches, and are therefore not concerned with the queue, are equally anxious to be in the front of the rush. On one occasion there was some kind of mistake, and the cloakrooms did not get unlocked until a minute or so after one; the anger and dismay caused would have seemed to the outsider quite fantastic. At five to one, as usual, all the girls who had not managed to wangle washing their hands earlier, gathered round the door of the cloakroom, and started as usual to yell for "Popeye"—the little ginger-headed man responsible for locking and unlocking the doors. For the first minute or two his non-appearance was treated rather as a joke, and there was a lot of laughter among the shouting:

"Come on, Popeye. You mustn't keep a lady waiting!"
"Come on, Popeye!"
"What's he doing?"
"He's gone to bed. Shall we come and wake you up, Popeye?"
"He's scared. He's scared we'll bugger him. Come on Popeye, we won't hurt you."
"Popeye! Hurry, Popeye, we're waiting."

But as five minutes passed and one o'clock drew near the joking ceased, and genuine anger took its place; when the

[1] The Ministry of Labour required standard is one wash-basin per twenty-five employees, and in sections where there are many more wash basins, the same phenomena is to be observed. Recently a strong personal appeal was made by the W.M. for less slacking in the interests of War production. There has not yet been sufficient time to see the result of the appeal (See notes in Appendix on shift working and general morale)—(*Works Manager*).

buzzer actually sounded and he still hadn't appeared, there were such shrieks of despair and fury as I have rarely heard. When, some two minutes later, Popeye appeared, the situation was such that he remained at a distance, threw the key into the middle of the crowd, and fled.[1]

The dinner hour is spent by most people in the canteen (the canteen itself is described elsewhere), knitting, sewing, and occasionally reading. If it is fine, quite a number go for strolls in the grounds, or outside, up and down the road. Work starts again at two o'clock, and we have to clock in for it as at the beginning of the day. There is not the same clocking-in rush, however, as a lot of people drift in singly and go on with their knitting or whatever it is, in little groups by the benches.

It is this stretch of time, from two o'clock till six (when there is a half-hour break for tea) that nearly everyone dreads. There is often quite a lot of talk about it among the girls coming in at the end of the dinner door:

> "Oh, I'm browned off! Think of it, till six o'clock!"
>
> "It's wicked! Think of it in the summer, with the sun shining and all outside! It'll kill me."
>
> "I could lie down and go to sleep. I feel like that—you know."
>
> "It drags terrible, this time to six o'clock."
>
> "I wish it was six o'clock now."
>
> "I wish it was Friday."
>
> "Back to slavery!" (This is a phrase quite often used, half jokingly, by the more C-class girls as they come back from dinner.)[2]

[1] "Popeye" is actually the Shop Steward and Workers' Representative for the Shop in question. He is an old London worker evacuated in the blitz. It was he who put forward the suggestion, at a Works Committee Meeting called to discuss time wasting due to washing, that the doors should be locked at half an hour to meal times and opened five minutes before time, which five-minute period would be legitimate time off for washing. He offered to take charge of the key and to some extent this attitude of the workers to their chosen representative is typical of the whole. The man in question is usually very critical of the Management and quick to stand up for workers' rights, but on this one occasion when he attempted to induce some idea of responsibility into the workers of the department, he was disowned on the spot. His responsibility was apparently "one way"—(*Works Manager*).

[2] Music-While-You-Work is indicated here to relieve the long dull period. It has now been introduced to coincide with the BBC broadcast, 10.30–11 a.m. and 3.0–3.30 p.m. The worker's reaction has not yet been ascertained.

LATER: Music-While-You-Work is very popular. Workers very keen and appreciate—(*Labour Manager*).

And certainly the time from two o'clock till six seems to go slowly. At about three o'clock one gets the feeling that the time will *never* pass; you think to yourself: after a whole hour, it will still only be four o'clock, and there will be two more hours to go after that. . . . A bewildering sense of helplessness comes over one; nothing one does *can* ever make a time as long as that pass. One gets the feeling that the time isn't passing on its own at all; that one has to drag the clock hand round the minutes by will-power. One begins to make idiotic bargains with oneself: if I drill a hundred of these holes without looking up, then by the time I do look up five minutes will have passed.

Between three and five in the afternoon more slacking and idling goes on than one would have thought possible in a war-time factory. Sometimes one can look along the bench and see not more than one girl in four actually working. But the others are rarely doing anything that could be definitely picked on by a foreman, such as knitting or reading. One will be sitting with her hand on the handle of her machine, as if just about to pull it down, and yet somehow not doing it; another will be patting her hair; another staring for the moment out of the window; another just settling down after a visit to the cloakroom, and so on.

It is at this hour that the activities known to the authorities as "lavatory-mongering" are at their height. People drift out to the cloakroom, and stay there for half an hour or more, eating sandwiches, talking, reading, and often just doing nothing at all. And this in spite of the fact that the cloakroom is most uninviting, containing simply three basins, two lavatories, and a few square feet of stone floor. There are no chairs or benches to sit on, not even a ledge on which to lay a bag or comb. Anything is welcome, so long as it provides a change from sitting at the bench.[1]

Now and then sporadic bursts of singing start in some part of the room or other and continue for a few minutes. It is usually a purely local affair, confined to the occupants of a few square yards of bench—nothing approaching community singing throughout the room ever develops. At this time (February) the songs most frequently heard were "Rose O'Day" and "Roll Out the Barrel". Singing seemed to be a symptom

[1] The foregoing seems to indicate complete failure of our action *re* the Machine Shop cloakroom taken on the Workers' suggestion. If the accommodation was more luxurious, the position would probably be worse. Lavatory-mongering has been a common element of time-wasting over a long period—(*Labour Manager*).

of boredom more than exuberance, as it occurred mostly during the dead period of ordinary weekday afternoons (three to five), and only rarely on Saturdays, or at the end of a spell of work.

After five o'clock there is a marked recovery in both cheerfulness and concentration on the job. The feeling that a break (tea at six o'clock) is in sight has a definitely stimulating effect. One feels that the worst is over, because the time after tea, from half-past six till eight, seems, for some reason, to fly past at extraordinary speed. Everyone feels this; it was remarked on spontaneously by a variety of girls, even before noticed by investigation. On the first day at tea, a girl said consolingly to a newcomer:

"You'll be all right now, the time goes ever so quick after tea."

"That's right," said her friend. "It goes lovely after tea. Funny, isn't it? It never drags, not after teatime."

It was quite true, we found; and it never failed. Sometimes after a particularly long afternoon one used to feel sure that *this* time it would go slowly after tea too. But somehow it never did. Eight o'clock always arrived as something of a surprise, just as one was feeling (for the first time since ten in the morning) that one wouldn't mind going on for another hour or so.

For clocking out in the evening there is some attempt at a queue, instead of a mere scramble. People line up round the wall of the room in something approaching the order in which they were ready, though the ruling is very loose, and some may slip in near the front without arousing much protest.

4

THE MACHINE-SHOP GIRLS

BEFORE GOING ON to discuss in detail the attitudes and feelings of the workers about their job and about the life they have to lead, it will be well to give some kind of picture of the girls and women employed here; of their characters, homes and background.

The majority of them are D-class country girls, with no experience whatever of industrial work, or indeed of any organised work in a community. A large proportion of them were domestic servants before they came here. A few had done done no work of any kind, other than housework in their own homes.

But perhaps better than generalisations, a few sketches of some typical machine-shop workers will illustrate the salient points:

I. HILDA

Hilda is a heavy, plain girl of about twenty-eight. She has a large pasty face, glasses, and dark hair cut in a bob and drawn off her face with a slide, like a schoolgirl. Her home is in a nearby town, where her people keep a public house, and until this year she worked as a domestic servant in a house. She was registered with the 28's, and put into this factory by the Ministry of Labour, and she accepts the situation with placid indifference. She is working on one of the handpresses on the back bench of the machine shop, and is one of the few who never seem to get bored with the job. She sits there, stolidly pushing the handle round hour after hour, looking rather vacantly in front of her. She says she "doesn't mind" the work here, just as she "didn't mind" her former job as a domestic servant, and has no further views about either of them. Her chief interest in life at the moment is her knitting. She and her mother belong to a knitting party in their town, and between them they are knitting a scarf in garter stitch for the Merchant Navy. Every day Hilda brings it to work with her and knits slowly but eagerly through all the breaks—she is not one of those who get on with their knitting under the bench or out in the cloakroom during working hours. She always tries to get ten rows done during the day, because she and her mother have worked out that if she does ten rows at work every day, and then brings it home for her mother to do a few more in the evening, they will get it done in time for Easter. Only on Mondays she is at a loss, and sits doing nothing during the breaks, because Monday is the day when the knitting party meets in the afternoon, and Hilda's mother likes to have the scarf to take to it.

She does not feel the lack of leisure as many of the girls do. She says:

> "Some of them grumble, but I don't mind. I've got nothing to do weekends, my mother sees to everything, she does my mending and all. I just do a bit of knitting, or I might go out for a walk Sunday afternoon. Sometimes my mum goes to church mornings, and then I might go with her."

She is as phlegmatic about her food as about everything else. Every day she brings a tin of sandwiches prepared by her mother and eats stolidly through them—eight for dinner and four for tea—without seeming much aware of what she is eating. On two occasions a neighbour was heard to ask her what was in them; both times the answer was: "I don't know. My mum does them." She does not, like most of the girls, draw on them for odd snacks during working hours.

She has no special friend, but is as good-natured as she is stupid, and is willing to talk to anyone who talks to her, making no difference in her manner in talking to people she has never seen before and talking to those who sit next her every day.

Altogether, she is one of the most contented of the machine-shop girls, and probably one of the best at her work.

2. PEGGY

Peggy is a lively, very good-looking girl of twenty, with lovely naturally-wavy hair, which she wears loose on her shoulders. She is the eldest of a family of eight, and is always in boisterous high spirits, and keeps her section of the bench in a constant state of laughter and chatter. She started her working life as a cinema usherette—she describes it enthusiastically as "a lovely job"—registered with the 20's last spring, and since then appears to have been shifted around by the Ministry of Labour to a number of different factories, ending up with this one. She has disliked the work in all of them equally, but natural high spirits enable her to treat the whole thing as a huge joke, and she has a completely carefree, happy-go-lucky attitude towards conscription, work, penalties, and all the rest of it. On every possible evening she gets off at half-past five (this can be done officially on one night a week, but with a little guile and complete disregard for risks and penalties of every kind, can actually be done a great deal oftener) and goes off with a crowd of friends, who with much shrieking and laughing and waving, manage to secure lifts to where she lives. Once home on these evenings, she usually goes to some dance or other, which involves staying up till two in the morning; and as she has to be up at six to catch the bus to work, it is not surprising that she often fails to catch it, and thus has a day off. Threats and warnings from the authorities have no effect on her whatever, except to provide food for the entertainment of her neighbours on the bench. One Saturday morning she came rushing down from the office practically hysterical with laughter:

"I went up there, I knew they were going to tell me off about last night, and he was sitting there, all so solemn—like this!—I was in fits, I couldn't hardly keep myself in. And he said to me—(becomes inaudible in new fit of laughing) he said to me I could be sent to prison next time. Sent to prison! (collapses with laughter). Me in prison picking—what is it? Me in prison picking okum! Can't you see me? Oh, I could have died! And him sitting there so solemn, thinking he was scaring me! Oh! I nearly told him, I wouldn't mind going to prison. Where are we now, I wanted to ask him? Isn't this a prison? Can't do what we like, can't go where we like. Oh, but you should have seen him!"

Story fades out in renewed bursts of laughter, in which, by now, everyone else is joining. The work itself bores her intensely, and her slapdash manner with the machine results in frequent breaking of drills—always an occasion for laughter, as her broken drills have become a standing joke.[1]

In the same carefree spirit, she always wears nice dresses and stockings to work, regardless of the fact that among the dirt and oil of the machine shop they are going to be ruined very quickly. Asked how she will manage about coupons, she says gaily:

"Oh, I don't know, I expect my brother will give me some. I'm not going to come in slops for anybody. I've always worn nice things to work, and *they* aren't going to stop me."

3. EDITH

A very sweet, gentle girl of twenty-two, small and very pretty. She is married and has two babies, and only came to work

[1] This confirms previous evidence of insufficient training in the Shops; some of these jobs are of the very simplest. The Foreman most likely assumes that the common sense of the matter would be obvious to the most ignorant, but apparently it is not enough, and amongst some girls there is a definite fear that they will be unable to carry out the job given to them, with consequent nervousness. The lack of adequate supervisory staff used to training new labour is a great handicap, but such grades have been almost impossible to obtain since the outbreak of war. The fact is, that the employee must know that these most important small tools are difficult to obtain, and in any case involve labour and material which the country can ill afford. The fact that there is no public condemnation of such wastage of national assets is in itself a reflection on the general attitude of the worker—(*Works Manager*).

here, she says, "To occupy my time, I was getting so miserable sitting home and worrying about Bill." Bill is her husband, serving with the R.A.F. somewhere out East. She didn't know where he was, and only rarely heard from him, and was very worried that he might be out in Singapore (during the period of the Singapore crisis). She thinks of and worries about him continually; carries photographs which she shows to us all at odd times, and talks continually of him:

> "When my husband was home he used to make such a fuss of us, me and my little girl. He'd bring us tea in bed and breakfast with toast before he went to work. I never used to get up for breakfast when he was home. And do you know, I never cleaned a window since I was married? He did all that. Wonderful in the house, he was; a wonderful husband. One of the best."

Sometimes she speaks bitterly of the war which has caused their separation:

> "I know we've got to win the war and all that, but it seems wicked, somehow, to take the fathers away like that. My little boy was only three months when his Daddy went out. If anything should happen to him, he'll never know his Daddy, and my little girl won't remember him. They ought to think a bit, and send out the single fellows. It's not myself I'm thinking of, it's the children. If a child's lost one of its parents it's lost everything."

She begs us all to be sure and listen on March 27th, when Sandy Mac. will be playing "Home Sweet Home Again" for him. She says:

> "Every time I listen to those programmes I cry. You hear the women giving the messages to their husbands on Wednesday night, and they can't hardly get through it sometimes; you can hear they're crying."

When I knew her she had been at the factory for about six weeks, and had decided to leave, as she found the hours too long and tiring; and though her sister was looking after the babies and the house for her, she didn't like being away so long every day:

"I know she does everything for them, but I never seem to see my babies now. I miss it, dressing them and feeding them, and I sort of feel they'll forget I'm their Mummy—you know what I mean. Starting at six in the morning and getting back at nine, all I see of them is when they're asleep."

She says also that her husband doesn't know she is working:

"He'd have a fit if he knew I was here. He told me when he left, whatever I did I wasn't to go out to work in a factory. He was frightened it would be too much for me."

She disliked the work, finding it dirtier and more monotonous than she had expected, but being by temperament very conscientious, did not do it badly or try to dodge it.

4. CLARIE

Clarie is fifteen, though she might easily be taken for twenty, she is so tall and well developed. She is the youngest but one of a large family of sisters living locally, and she has worked in the factory for nearly a year. She does not seem to be a bad worker, but is invariably so tired and sleepy that it is hard to tell what her real potentialities are. The main reason for this is that she goes around with a young man of twenty-five or more, who takes her about to dances, socials, pictures, etc., in and outside the town, practically every evening, and she rarely gets to bed before one or two in the morning. At her age this tells on her pretty heavily—a thing which he does not seem to realise, but treats her in every way as if she were a woman of his own age. He is the charge-hand on the bench where she works, so every evening she stays till eight o'clock (being under eighteen she may work until only half-past five) so as to walk home with him—also so as to prevent him flirting with any of the other girls, which he usually does whenever she is not there.

One way and another, it is a very wearing life for her. Quite apart from the complication of the young man, she is much younger than most of the other girls and finds it difficult to get on with them. Most of them regard her as a rather silly, sulky child, and leave her to herself; and there is now the added fact that anyone who gets off with an authority of any kind, even a charge-hand, is usually looked on slightly askance by the others.

5. MOLLY

A queer, old-fashioned looking little thing, with glasses, and a rather high, childlike voice. The way she wears her clothes and her hair makes her look well over thirty, though actually she is twenty-four. She is usually working on one of the drilling machines, and she is almost the only girl there who really and positively enjoys the work, for its own sake, and not because of the wages, or companionship, or patriotism or anything else. Her particular job is just as dull as anyone else's, and yet she talks about it with real enthusiasm—she will rush up to you during a break and describe just what kind of part she is drilling now, how fast she can do them, what the charge-hand said when he saw how many she had done:

> "A lovely job I've got to-day," she will say eagerly. "Nice clean little brass parts, the drill goes through them lovely. Oh, I'm enjoying it. I did a thousand of them before eleven o'clock, and I called Lou (the charge-hand) and showed him what I'd done, and he was ever so surprised."

She never joins in the fierce rushes at dinner time and the end of the day. She usually stays at her machine until the buzzer has actually sounded, and the others are tearing for the canteen; she then goes in a leisurely way to the now empty cloakroom, and only goes up to the canteen when the rush and queue have subsided:

> "I don't believe in all this rushing," she says. "You don't get things any quicker. I get my dinner just as good as anyone else when I go quietly after they've all got theirs."

Technically speaking, Molly is a conscript, called up with the 24's, but really the manner of her coming was much more that of a volunteer. It seems that when she registered she was in service, working as parlourmaid in a fair-sized country house. When it came to the registration of women, her employer was very anxious not to let her go:

> "She sent for me, and she seemed very upset, and she said: 'We can't let them take you, Molly,' and she told me, 'Tell them you've got bad eyesight; tell them this and tell

them that.' Well I'd told her I wanted to go into war work, but she wouldn't listen, she said, 'No, you tell them you've got bad eyesight, you'd never stand the strain. You're not strong enough, Molly,' she told me. Well, then the Labour Exchange sent for me to come on the 9th, but my lady said to me, 'Tell them you can't go so soon; get them to put it off.' I told her I didn't think they'd do that, and so she said she'd phone them up. So she did, and when I went round there the girl said all right, they'd change it for me. But I told the girl, I said: 'Please don't change it. I want to go into a factory, but Mrs. B. doesn't want me to go. I'd rather you didn't change it.' So she wrote to Mrs. B. that they couldn't change it, I'd have to come, but she never told Mrs. B. I'd asked her to say so. It was very nice of her, wasn't it, don't you think so?

"Mrs. B. was very angry, but she had to let me go. She kind of guessed, I think, she knew I wanted to go into a factory. She said I'd let her down. She told me: 'If you go to that factory you're a fool, and a big one. It will ruin your eyes, and you'll never stand it. You'll be sorry, I warn you. The wages may sound big, she told me, but by the time you've paid for your food and your lodgings you'll have less than you're getting here.'

"So I wrote to her the other day, and I told her that for ruining my eyes, I do all my work here without looking at it. It was cleaning your silver, I said, ruined my eyes, not this work. I told her that I'm ever so happy, and my board is tiny, and I spend an average of 9d. a day in the canteen. I'm putting away as much as I got altogether with her. Now the cook's left too, she's gone to a factory in London, so I don't know how she'll manage."[1]

Molly has no close friends in the factory or in the town, and she hardly ever goes out anywhere in the evening. She is billeted with an elderly landlady who specially asked for someone who was quiet, and would not go out much in the evening. Molly prides herself on being this sort of person:

[1] This attitude is typical of many mistresses. In one case a householder actually wrote to her M.P. twice in an endeavour to retain the services of a maid. The girl was browbeaten and had to be actually threatened with prosecution by the Ministry of Labour with the possibility of a £100 fine, before she could be persuaded by the Labour Exchange to ignore her mistress and actually report for duty—(*Works Manager*).

"I'm not one for rushing about like some of these girls. When I've finished work I like to go home and stop there. A real little home, that's where I asked them to put me. I can't understand why some of them want to be out all the time. You'd have thought they'd be tired, wouldn't you? Just rush in and change their dress and rush out again, every single night. It would kill me. But there's terrible rumours going round about some of them. They don't get in till two in the morning—that sort of thing."

The only social event she goes to is the Sunday afternoon tea run by her chapel. Again she has not made many friends here, but she seems to enjoy going. Apart from that, she spends her evenings writing letters, sewing, and reading. Molly reads far more than most of the girls—she always brings a book to read in the canteen. She does not just read idly for pleasure, but has a real thought-out attitude toward it, and regards it as a worthwhile occupation. At the time of writing she is reading *A Tale of Two Cities*, and intends to have read the whole of Dickens by the end of the summer.

Though her appearance is rather dowdy and old-fashioned, she gives her clothes a lot of thought and planning, in a rather anxious, prim sort of way. Factory life has confronted her with a lot of new clothes problems, which she described one day as follows:

"It's so difficult. I can't decide what to do for the summer, I want to save my cotton dresses, I don't want to wear them to work, they'll get filthy. Are those slacks very hot? I did think of those—I think they're all right if you're on war work, don't you? I don't think they're nice for girls in the ordinary way. Or I might buy a skirt, and wear one of those dark shirt blouses with it. I want something to look nice coming home, it will be the sun out when we come out then, but I don't want to spoil my nice things at work. It's difficult. I won't go home looking like *anything*. I wouldn't go home looking like *that*, for instance (indicates girl walking in front of us dressed in shabby, shapeless coat, bare legs, broken shoes); but we won't mention any names.

"It's terrible the way the dirt gets through on to your clothes. I was ashamed of my petticoat this week, it was all quite black. I'm used to nice things, you know. I was brought up to think more of my under things than my top ones. We used to put on all clean things, right the way down, every other day. My mother always used to say, suppose you were run over, in the street, and they took you to hospital, you wouldn't want to feel ashamed, would you? I always think of that when I put my clothes on in the morning."

Although she seems to lead such a dull life, Molly is one of the happiest, most contented girls in the factory. She sums it up herself:

"I'm happy here because I put my heart into it. If I was always trying how little I could do like some of them, I'd be fed up like the rest of you. But I'm always like that. If it's only mending a stocking, I put my heart into it, and I can enjoy it. People laugh at me, they say 'Why don't you go out and enjoy yourself, Molly?' And I say, I *am* enjoying myself. Whatever you see me doing, you know I'm enjoying it. That's why."

6. SADIE

Sadie is usually working on one of the hand-presses. She is a slow, very good-natured girl, with a round red face and dark hair. When she is in the mood, she can work efficiently and untiringly; but most of the time she is not in the mood at all, and dawdles most of the day. She will sit for minutes on end gazing round the room; or she will get up and wander over to a neighbour, flop down with her elbows on the neighbour's bench, to stay there talking until noticed by foreman or charge-hand. Then she will go back to her place, give the press a few turns, stop once more, and yawn, or look through her handbag, or merely fidget and play with the parts she is working on, instead of putting them into the press. She is well liked by the other girls, because she is always in a good temper, always ready to talk to anybody, whether they are friends of hers or not, and is generous with sweets, cigarettes, and anything else she may happen to possess.

She is an only child of poor country people, living in a cottage a mile or so outside a nearby town. Thus she has half an hour's walk before she gets the bus in the town, and has to leave the house at half-past six in the morning and does not get back till half-past nine at night. She resents the lack of leisure. Before she came here she worked in a greengrocer's shop, where she managed to have a good deal of time to herself:

"I loved that job. It was just the man and his wife running it, and they were ever so good to me. If there wasn't much to do they used to say, 'You go off home, Sadie, we can manage,' and I'd go out into the sunshine—oh, I did love it. Sometimes I'd been on my own there all day, and if there wasn't much doing I'd have my knitting, and just get on quietly, do what there was to do. Sometimes it was very busy, Saturdays and that, but I didn't mind. We finished at five or half-past most afternoons, and I could meet my boy when he got back, and we'd go to the pictures or anything like that.

"It's wicked the hours we work here. I don't know any other factory works like we do. I know they don't where my boy works, they finish at half-past five like in peace time. He's got nothing to do all the time till I get back, and I don't get in till half-past nine. Even if I miss my supper it doesn't give you much time, does it, not if you have to be up at six in the morning. I can't hardly get myself out of bed some mornings; they have to regular knock me about to get me up, and I always want a nap in the afternoon. I could lay my head down on the bench this minute, and not wake up till eight o'clock. I could, honest."

Sadie is twenty, but wasn't called up until December, because her previous job was in a food shop. Her resentment at being sent here is increased by her parents, who tell her that the hours are too long, that it is ruining her health, and that it is wrong for women to be conscripted. Her mother also complains of missing Sadie's help in the house—in which an airman and his wife are billeted. Sadie herself dislikes the work as well as the long hours, and is counting the days till she can leave in a much more definite way than most of them:

"The day the war ends I'll be the first out of this factory. It'll be a race, and I'll be the one to get to the outside of those gates the first."[1]

[1] One of the principal conclusions from this section is that the heavier, more solid type of girl, preferably the older type, is more suited for Machine Shop work of this nature, unless younger employees are definitely interested in mechanical production (as some girls actually are). Now that the period of expansion is over, there would appear to be need for more fitting of square pegs into square holes—(*Labour Manager*).

5

THEIR ATTITUDE TO THE WORK

It is clear enough from the preceding sections that in the machine shop as a whole there is little interest in the work. The main preoccupation is how to make the time between breaks pass as quickly as possible, and to wait for the evening to come. "Roll on, eight o'clock" is a phrase heard over and over again during the course of the day, in all parts of the room. Some of the girls are very conscious of this preoccupation of theirs, and one often hears quite long conversations on the subject of how quickly or slowly the time is going on a given day (and it is a curious fact that there is almost always unanimous agreement about whether a given stretch of time has gone quickly or slowly):

"It went quick this morning, didn't it?"

"Yes, it went lovely and quick between eleven and twelve, but it dragged after that, I thought."

"Yes, just after the twelve o'clock buzzer. It started to drag then."

"Funny, wasn't it? It usually goes so quick after the twelve o'clock buzzer."

"I hope it will go as quick this afternoon."

"Hope so. You can always tell, can't you? If it goes quick up to half-past two, then it's going to go quick all the afternoon."

"It's funny, that."

To some extent this intense interest in the passing of time serves as substitute for interest in the work, but it has a curious psychological effect. At the end of the day one tends to feel not tired, but as if one hasn't had a day at all—has missed it somehow—coming out into the blackout one gets a sort of angry shock of surprise to find it is night again already, when it seems that it ought still to be fairly soon after breakfast, so little has happened in the interval. And somewhat the same thing happens on a larger scale as the weeks go by. An intelligent C-class girl of twenty-five who has been here for two years comments:

"It's funny, when you're in there the time goes so slow you think it will never be eight o'clock; but somehow when you look back the weeks seem to fly by. I've been here two years, but I sometimes feel I've only been here a few weeks. It gives me quite a nasty sort of feeling, like it's running away with my life, you know what I mean?"

But this attitude of passive waiting for the day to be over does not imply merely lack of interest in the actual jobs to be done. It implies also a profound and very significant reluctance to accept the twelve hours spent in the factory as part of real life at all; it is simply a blank patch between one brief evening and the next. It means that it is going to be extremely difficult to rouse *any* kind of corporate attitude to anything, whether it be social activities (and the management have made earnest efforts to make the factory a centre of social life as well as a place for work), criticisms and complaints, political activity, or anything else. This apathy about the factory and everything to do with it is about the biggest problem with which the authorities are faced, and it lies at the bottom of most of the difficulties which we shall now discuss.

(I) LACK OF UNDERSTANDING OF THE WORK

To some extent this is, of course, inevitable, as much of the apparatus made is of a secret, as well as of a highly technical, nature. But not only do most of the machine-shop girls not understand what they are making, but most of them have not the faintest desire to understand. Only on very rare occasions, and from particular types of girl, was there any spontaneous reference to what a given part might be used for, even from the most limited point of view. For instance, an ordinary intelligent girl of about twenty has been working for several months on one of the "tapping" machines (i.e. a machine for putting the thread into a hole so that it will take a screw); and after having spent months turning out tens of thousands of these threaded holes, she still had not the faintest idea of what difference her operation was making to the whole. *She had never once picked up one of those parts after she had done, and seen that the hole now had a thread in it which it hadn't when she put it into the machine.*'[1]

[1] Further exhibitions of finished equipment and a clear explanation of all the parts manufactured would help—(*Labour Manager*).

Yes, agreed, but interest is best aroused by the work itself. We have many examples in the Shop in question of girls without any previous mechanical experience, actually doing their own setting up and operating with little or

It is interesting that older women usually have a much clearer idea of what they are doing than the younger ones in this sort of way. For instance, a middle-aged D-class woman, working on one of the drilling machines, describes a job she has done:

> "One time I had some little tiny screws to drill, little devils they were. I broke six drills on them at the start. But in the end I got into it, and I did 1,500 of them. He was so surprised, he said it was trained work, but I said: 'That's all right, when I get into it.' He said he would always give them to me to do. I was as good as a trained worker. You see they have to be just exactly right, or they don't fit. I don't understand it, of course, but they've got to fit, just exact where they have to go, or it will all be put out, kind of thing."

Interest in the way the machines work is also rare, and when it does appear is generally in older women also:

> "I asked my husband why they call this a 'tapping' machine and not drilling—because it is a kind of drill, really, you'd think. He told me the tapping is for the screw—the round-and-round hole. But I still don't see why 'tapping'. You'd have thought 'screwing' or something, wouldn't you?"

The younger girls have all accepted the obscure word "tapping" without a query.

A short time ago the interesting experiment was made of showing an exhibition of finished sets in the canteen, so that the machine-shop girls could come and see what it was that they were contributing to make. Up to a point, the exhibition was a great success. The girls gathered round the sets, and many of them looked eagerly for their own parts, and showed great excitement when they found them. One felt that their interest was personal rather than mechanical; that they did not care how or why the part fitted on where it did, but that they had

---

no supervision. These girls are, of course, rapidly promoted, but in the first place it should be noted that the interest was shown by the employee and was not the result of external pressure. The tendency should be for those definitely not interested in the work as such, to be put on operations in this or other departments, not involving the use of machinery, but mainly consisting of very elementary assembly functions—(*Works Manager*).

a strong feeling of being personally complimented on their work—rather like the feeling of seeing one's name in print. Partly, too, it was the external excitement of seeing a familiar thing in unexpected surroundings, like finding your own old hat in a jumble sale. But undoubtedly the exhibition did rouse a certain amount of real interest in the work itself, which was certainly not there before, and it was a pity that it was impossible to follow up its results more closely, as it took place at the very end of this investigation.[1]

(II) LACK OF INTEREST IN WORKING FOR THE WAR EFFORT

It is felt by the management that one of the big problems of this type of factory is that the work seems superficially to be so remote from the war; that it is not of obvious immediate use, like making bullets and shells. They feel that lack of interest in the work is largely due to this—that the girls do not feel they are contributing directly to the war. And a good deal of trouble has been taken (including the exhibition mentioned above) to emphasise and publicise the importance of the work for the war effort.

As far as the machine shop is concerned, however, evidence goes to show that some of this anxiety is misdirected. The trouble there is not that the girls do not realise that their work is important to the war, but that the majority of them are so little *interested in the war that they do not care whether their work is important to it or not.* As in so many country places, to the women at least, the war is simply a thing that happens, like a thunderstorm or an earthquake, and victory is similarly a thing that will happen. All that can be done is to hope that it will happen soon, as one hopes for fine weather. The idea that anything one does or doesn't do oneself can possibly have any bearing on it all, comes very slowly.

This attitude to the war was illustrated by a small study of newspaper reading in the canteen. Every day for a fortnight at the end of February, an observer brought a copy of the

[1] This is being repeated at regular intervals. In addition we recently arranged for workers to visit a warship fitted with gear made at the factory. The party was elected by Shop ballot and made the visit unaccompanied by representatives of the Management (Production). The party was given a royal welcome by the officers and men, and returned full of enthusiasm at having seen instruments actually made by them fitted in one of H.M. ships. Efforts should be made to repeat this sort of thing, but secrecy regulations make it difficult—(*Works Manager*).

Daily Mirror into the canteen and handed it round among immediate neighbours (about a dozen usually had some kind of a look at it), and noted down afterwards all the items in the paper that had attracted any comments of any kind. During the whole of this period there was a total of not more than four remarks about the war news at all, and these were of the briefest. Here is a typical set of reactions to looking at the paper—the particular day being February 26th, the day when a Cripps speech was headlined all over the front page:

"What's your birthday, Peg?"
"June. First half of June. What's it say?"
"'No great excitements, but a pleasant, easy-going sort of day.'"
"(*Laughs*) Easy-going! I work till eight o'clock, and don't get home till half-past nine! Good thing they say there's no excitement, anyway."
"What's yours, Lil?"

And so on, until the birthdays of most of the girls within hearing have been accounted for. Then they start looking at the other pages:

"Isn't that a nice one? Look, the Queen talking to someone in a factory. It's nice, isn't it. It flatters her."
"What's that about the A.T.S. pyjamas? They don't get no coupons, do they, in the A.T.S.?"
"It says they can get them without now, or something. I wouldn't mind being in the A.T.S., would you? Better than here."[1]

Interest flags, and there is no more talk about the paper. One girl goes on looking languidly up and down the middle page until one of the men from another table comes and borrows it.

This negative attitude to the war is to a large extent characteristic of all country districts, but it is even more strongly marked among factory workers like these than among the rest of the population in the area. For, paradoxical as it may seem,

[1] When we are able, we should initiate broadcast news bulletins as a regular feature—(*Labour Manager*).

I disagree. People must be interested in the War first and then they will want to listen to news bulletins. When we had a wireless set in the Canteen, not one person in twenty bothered to listen to the news—(*Works Manager*).

life in a twelve-hours-a-day war factory makes one feel further removed from the war than one could in any other type of life.[1]

It is hard for anyone who has not tried it, to realise the curious, almost exhilarating sense of the slipping away of all responsibilities that comes over people after a few days in this sort of work. From eight in the morning till eight at night life is taken off one's own hands, completely and absolutely. All personal and social claims and responsibilities have vanished; and, in these lower grades of work, no alternative responsibility for the work itself emerges. And it does not stop here. When a girl gets home at half-past eight or nine at night, what awaits her? Someone else has, of necessity, coped with the rationing and shopping problems; someone else has tidied the house, planned to-morrow's meals, done the washing. Someone else has seen that the rent and milk bill have been paid; someone else has probably written any letters that need to be written. All that the average girl has to cope with when she gets home (because this is about all she has physically the time to cope with) is getting undressed and putting the curlers in her hair. This situation will be discussed in detail later; the point for the moment is this. Is it surprising that, after a few weeks of this sort of life, a girl should begin to feel isolated from the outside world, and lose her sense of responsibility towards it? By the nature of her work and its long hours, she is cut off from the daily life of her community; she is sheltered from its day to day difficulties and problems (i.e. rationing, transport, etc.). The attitude which she inevitably develops to life as a whole colours even more markedly her attitude to the war. It is a well-known fact that the average working-class woman's interest in the war is kept alive, not so much by the large-scale tragedies, like the loss of this, that or the other piece of territory, but by the personal inconveniences: rationing, blackout, shortages and so on. And from these inconveniences someone who works in a war factory, with an adequate canteen, for twelve hours a day, is automatically excluded. There is nothing left to keep alive in her even the slightest degree of interest, which her mother and sisters feel in the war.

This, then, is probably the main reason for the almost complete lack of war feeling which characterises the machine shop.

[1] It is this lack of interest in the War effort which the Management definitely failed to appreciate and take into account. They are still unable to cope with it. It is a problem outside the factory itself and is enlarged upon in the Appendix.

Never once, from any of the girls, was there any suggestion that we ought to do this or that because of the war; never was there any shadow of public opinion directed against slacking or dodging of any kind. Expert dodgers are merely envied for their ability to get away with it.[1]

Public opinion is indeed such that anything which interrupts work, even for a few moments, is acclaimed with unrestrained delight. One morning the electricity which drives the machines kept on suddenly going off for a few minutes; and every time this happened a spontaneous shout of "Hurray!" went up all over the room; and corresponding groans as soon as it started again. Never was there any suggestion that it mattered that time was being wasted and production held up. And on another morning, when for two hours the electricity didn't go on at all, the only complaint heard was from those working on the hand-presses and other non-electric processes. They complained that it wasn't fair that they should have to work while the others didn't!

While the situation remains like this, appeals to patriotism as an incentive to increased production are almost valueless. The patriotic posters ("It all depends on me", "We want your help", etc., etc.) which plaster the walls of every room in the factory might as well be so much ornamental scroll work for all the notice that is taken of them, by the machine shop girls at least. As before, however, we must recognise a marked distinction between the younger girls, who form the bulk of the machine shop workers, and the sprinkling of older women. These older women do have some idea of and interest in the connection of their work with the war effort. From them occasional remarks are heard, like the following:

> "It's not bad. A bit monotonous. Still, you do feel it's helping the war, don't you?" (F45D)
>
> "My first week here I thought I'd never stick it. I thought 'I can't stick this.' But I got used to it. And I thought to myself: 'I'm lucky not to be getting bombs like some of the poor people. I ought to do something to help. I mustn't grumble'." (F.50D.[1])
>
> "If I was going in for factory work I'd like to do it properly—learn to do a more complicated job. You don't feel you're doing nothing like this. Of course, we know it helps, but you know what I mean—you don't *feel* you're doing anything." (F35C)

[1] The Production Committee should be used to arouse public opinion against dodgers—(*Labour Manager*).

It is probably not coincidence that it is just these older women who still hold some threads of responsibility for their own homes. Though they can't do much actual housework, they do still plan and arrange to some extent, what is to be done in their absence. They may be overtired as a result of this, but they do at least retain some vestiges of a normal life and outlook.

(III) LACK OF CORPORATE FEELING AT WORK

The main reason for this was indicated at the beginning of this section; it is just one of the symptoms of the general reluctance to put any heart or interest into any aspect of the factory life. But other smaller factors enter into it. One of these is that in the machine shop, with a few exceptions, *no one's work depends noticeably on anyone else's*. In most cases the work is brought from the store room, given to the girl to do, and then is taken away again; there is very little occasion to hand the same parts on from one girl to another, each performing a different operation on them. Occasionally it happens that a part has to go through two, or perhaps even three machine shop hands before it disappears, but this is not enough to create the spirit of corporate achievement which is possible in other parts of the factory, where the same parts have to pass down an entire bench, each girl adding to or altering them in some way.

There are a number of symptoms of this lack of corporate feeling, the most noticeable of which is the small amount of notice the girls take of each other, outside their immediate circle of friends. Though there are less than one hundred there, it is possible to ask a girl who has been there two years the name of another, who has also been there two years, and she will not know. Similarly there is considerably less gossip about each other's affairs than one would normally expect in such a gathering; most of the gossip and anecdotes one hears are about people known to the speakers *at home*, not in the factory. Another possibly significant point is the fact (noted earlier) that singing at work never spreads all through the room, but remains confined to the corner where it started. Sometimes, indeed, different parts of the room will be singing different songs at the same time.

(IV) FEELING OF INFERIORITY

Some of the girls are very conscious of their position in the machine shop. They feel they are looked down on by the rest of the factory—which to some extent is true, but not nearly as much so as some of them imagine. The machine shop certainly has the reputation of being very rough and unmannerly—C-class girls from other departments make remarks like these:

> "I wouldn't like to be in the machine shop; it's a very low class of girls you get there."
>
> "They always seem to be knocking at you among themselves; I never like going in there; you can sort of feel them staring at you."
>
> "Some of them are all right in there, but some of them are very low—real nasty some of them."

The machine shop girls tend to exaggerate the extent of this feeling, and many of them are very much on the defensive about it:

> "They think we're just dirt under their feet, but I'd like to know what would happen to this place if the machine shop was to stop for a week? It would stop the whole place."
>
> "Do you know what someone said to my sister? My sister told them I was in the machine shop, and they said: 'That's the most suitable place for her.' I was wild when I heard it. If I'd known who it was I'd have killed them, I would, really."
>
> "I should think so. Who was it, did you find out?"
>
> "No, my sister wouldn't tell me. She knew how wild I was."[1]

On one occasion the voice down the microphone that calls members of the staff to the telephone, made a slip at the beginning of the call, and instead of saying: "Calling Mr. C, please", started off "Calling the——" and then stopped, recovered itself and made the correct announcement. There was a general laugh at this, and one of the girls said:

> "I thought they were going to say: 'Calling the machine-shop scrubs, please; calling the machine-shop scrubs.' That's what they call us in the office. Machine-shop scrubs."

[1] I think it would be a useful experiment to try out a system of temporary transfers from department to department, including office workers. Employees would then appreciate the other person's job and it might tend to break down the queer class difference that crops up as between Shops and Departments—(*Labour Manager*).

Others react to the feeling of inferiority in another way, by belittling the machine shop themselves, and priding themselves on "not mixing" with the others:

> "I don't like the girls here," said a C-class woman of about thirty on my first morning. "They're very mixed. You'll see. This is the worst place to come to, I don't like it at all. I don't mix with any of them."

Another quiet, rather reserved girl of about twenty-five says:

> "I know I have to work here, and I can't get out, but I don't have much to do with the other girls. They aren't nice; they aren't the sort of girl I'm used to." (See later notes on machine-shop girls transferred to other sections.)

(v) COMPLAINTS AND CRITICISMS

Complaints actually voiced about concrete, specific subjects are exceedingly few; the whole attitude to the factory is too casual to breed anything but vague, undirected moaning and dislike. Such complaints as there are can be classified as follows:

(a) *Being here at all.*

Talk about possible ways and means of getting out is frequent, but few get so far as to take any practical steps to secure their release. A lot of people regret bitterly that they ever let themselves be put here:

> "I wish I'd volunteered for the A.T.S. when I could have done. You get more freedom there."
>
> "I'd never have come here, but I never knew they'd make me stop like this. I only wanted to be here for a bit to be near my Mum."

Perhaps one of the most vivid pictures in the minds of most of the machine-shop girls is the vision of the Last Day in the factory. Often and often it creeps into the talk, and sometimes one hears conversations like this, between two girls in their early twenties, both conscripts:

> "The day the war is over I'll be the first one out of here. I'll be down that path before they've finished announcing it."

"I wonder what they'll do. Will they call us all up to the canteen to announce it?"

"Most probably they won't tell you. Let you work the day so they don't lose their money's worth. That'd be their way."

"I'm not going to work the day out! When peace starts, I'm going, I don't care whether it's morning, afternoon or evening!"

Another girl breaks in:

"They'd make you work the day out; they can prevent you leaving before the end of the day."

"They can't, can they? Oh, they couldn't! Not when peace had been declared. They wouldn't do that, would they? They couldn't. We'd all walk out on them."

"Won't it be lovely if it's a lovely summer day and it happens dinner time. Like if peace was declared now, and we just put on our things and went home! I wouldn't clock out or anything, would you?"

Although dislike of being in the factory at all is far the most often voiced complaint, it is not exactly a grievance. The girls do not feel that they *ought* not to be made to stay here; they do not think of it in those sort of terms at all. It is simply a thing that has happened to them, and they dislike it, and so they complain, just as they might complain of the weather. There is only rarely any suggestion that someone ought to do something about it.

(b) *Long hours.*

Almost everyone feels that the hours are too long, but here again there is not much coherent idea that anything could or should be done about it. Objection to them is expressed simply by vague moaning, and by taking time off whenever and wherever possible. Complaints are focused on lack of leisure rather than tiredness:

"By the time you've had your supper and had a wash, it's time to go to bed."

"I can't ever go to a dance now. I like to have time to get ready, you know. You can't go straight from work. It makes you miserable, never able to get out in the evening."

"Just bed and work—that's all it comes to."

(c) *Break periods.*

Here and there among the aimless gloom about the four-hour stretch from two till six in the afternoon, were occasional explicit demands for a break during this period:

"It would make all the difference, wouldn't it, if we just had ten minutes to look forward to at half-past three."

"It's not fair, the Assembly girls have a teatime half through the afternoon, why shouldn't we have it?"[1]

(d) *Cloakroom.*

Complaints about the cloakroom are the only examples met at all frequently of definite grievance about a specific, limited subject. In point of fact, the cloakroom is far too small (three basins and two lavatories for over fifty people); but the complaints heard were not usually about this so much as about minor and irregular shortcomings like lack of soap, no hot water, wet and dirty towels:

"It's disgusting in here; if there's hot water there isn't soap and if there's soap there isn't hot water."

"It's not fair. They have hot water all the time in the Assembly, and theirs is clean work. We have the dirty work, we ought to have the hot water."

"They ought to change the towels at every break. Look at this! You can't touch them after ten in the morning."

But it illustrates the general apathy of the girls about their whole life here that, though these complaints were heard comparatively frequently, there was never any strong suggestion of trying to get the authorities to do anything about it. Even in the case of the bolt that had come off one of the lavatory doors, nobody seriously considered asking to have it replaced (which certainly would have been done). It was simply grumbled about and left at that.[2]

[1] Assembly Dept. takes its 10 mins. break in the morning, and Machine Shop in the afternoon in order to stagger the load on the canteen—(*Works Manager*).

[2] Hot water shortage is a real problem. It is largely due to our inability to educate workers to wash their hands in the right manner. Special compounds are provided to rub on the hands before starting work in order to wash them easily when dirty and greasy. In spite of many campaigns, employees will persist in putting it on after the grease and dirt have covered the skin, using it as a grease remover. The resultant mixture of soap, compound, dirt and grease is then very difficult to wash off under a tap and is wiped on to the towel. In spite of the provision on an average of one towel per ten persons per day, some of them have to be seen to be believed—(*Works Manager*).

6

MACHINE SHOP TO ASSEMBLY

THE FIRST IDEAS about the Assembly department came from a babel of angry talk in the machine-shop cloakroom one afternoon. Jenny, Lena and Eileen, all of whom had been in the machine shop for a year or more, had suddenly, on the previous day, been transferred to the Assembly—apparently as a punishment for idling and wasting time in the machine shop. All three were very much upset, and had come over to the machine shop during their tea break to air their grievance to a sympathetic crowd. From the confused buzz of conversation these remarks emerged clearly:

"It's not fair, is it, taking away girls who've been here two years. They're bringing in all these new girls in here, and throwing out the old ones. Why can't they put the new girls in the Assembly?"

"I wanted to tell him, if I'm not good enough for the machine shop after two years, then I'd like to have my cards back."

"I told him, I said I wanted to stop in the machine shop, and he said: 'I know you do, it's not my idea to move you'."

"Well, if it wasn't his idea why didn't he stop it? He's the manager."

"He said I've been staying too long in the cloakroom. I'm not the only one, I told him. I'd like to know who doesn't go in? At four o'clock there isn't room to get in. You can go and look for yourself, I said."

"There's someone been carrying tales to Mr. B. (the foreman), and I've got an idea who it is too. It's a mean thing, isn't it, go and tell Mr. B. who's in the cloakroom."

"He asked me about afternoons off. Afternoons off! I don't have any. I told him I'd had a weekend, and he said 'What! A weekend?' Yes, I said, I went to see my young man's mother. Then he asked me how many brothers I had in the Forces, and I said five. That held him. He couldn't say nothing then. I shouldn't think there's many girls here with five brothers in the Forces."[1]

[1] This is an interesting perversion of the truth. The girls were actually called into the W.M.'s office for a lecture before being transferred, thus hoping

"He said: 'Are you married, Miss J.?' Fancy asking that? Are you married *Miss* J. I wanted to tell him, if I was married I wouldn't be called Miss, would I?"

"It's awful in there (i.e. Assembly). You have to ask if you want to go to the toilet. Put your hand up like at school: 'Please, Miss, can I leave the room?' I'm going to bring a chamber pot, see what they say to that!"

"Dinner at twelve, it's too early. I'm not hungry at twelve. And we don't get no break in the morning, the time drags as bad as the afternoon, it does, really," (Lunch time is staggered).

"It's worse. It seems worse, somehow. It gets me down, having tea half-past five. The evening don't half drag after six. You know how lovely and quick it goes after tea here; it don't over there; it drags terrible."

"You're not allowed to talk, nothing, are you?" says one of the other girls in awed tones: "I've heard they aren't allowed to talk over Assembly."

"They can't stop *me* talking; needn't think they can."

"I started in the Assembly, but I hated it there. I didn't like it, I didn't like the supervisor. The others could do what they liked, but she was always after me: 'Sit round straight,' she used to say. That kind of thing."

"They're terrible snobbish over there. Turning up their noses because we come from the machine shop. I'd like to ask some of them where *they* come from. That would bring them down a bit, some of them."

All the girls were agreed that to be sent to the Assembly was in the nature of a tragedy. This seemed at first rather surprising, because the assembly work must be more interesting, and to be moved there in some sense a promotion. But a fortnight later something of the reasons for their dislike emerged, when an observer was herself transferred to Assembly.

The first impression was of a vast, low-roofed hall, out of reach of the daylight and lit eternally by white neon lights.

---

to cure some of the worst evils by removing the worst offenders. The particular girl in question was asked if she had any brothers in the Forces, and she answered, "Yes, five." She was then asked, "How would you feel if one of your brothers was short of equipment at a vital moment in a battle because you or some other slacker had not made it in time?" She hung her head in shame and almost burst into tears. The consequent show of bravado when getting back to her mates was the natural reaction—(*Works Manager*).

Running longways down it were lines of benches, covered with what seem at first sight to be thousands and thousands of coloured toys, like some fantastic Christmas shopping store. A closer look reveals that this effect is produced by all the many different coloured wires and plugs that are being used.

Even at first glance, one can see that the atmosphere is different from that of the machine shop. Many of the girls are engaged on elaborate and complicated work, demanding a good deal of attention. The slapdash, carefree atmosphere of the machine shop is replaced by one of purposeful attention—sometimes even of interest. The type of girl employed here is different too; C rather than D, with a liberal sprinkling of B's. Let the investigator tell the tale:

She was set to work beside a little C-class girl of about twenty. Hers was a particularly fiddling and difficult job, demanding fingers both small and strong, for wrestling with tiny but obstinate screws and fittings. She has worked at it for several months now, and is one of the few girls who can manage it. She says of it:

> "They've put me on easy jobs sometimes, but I like something to struggle with. I like going on and on until I've got it right, so when I'm finished I can think to myself— 'There, *I* did that! Aren't I a clever girl?'"

This sort of attitude—quite unknown in the machine shop—belongs in some degree to many of the girls here. The reason is simple. Instead of completely monotonous, repetition work, most of the girls here work on jobs which take twenty minutes or half an hour each, not just a few seconds; and most of them require a fair degree of at least manual skill, and also attention. Another very important factor is that (on the bench referred to at least) a set number is given for the day. Thus the whole bench is supposed to turn out say twenty a day, which means that each girl has to perform twenty of her operations. This gives one a totally different attitude to time. There is no longer the blind waiting for the time to pass, but rather a certain amount of directed effort to get the given job done in the given time. Not that there are any special penalties for not getting twenty done, but if one particular girl is being very slow over her part of the work, it means that the next girl, to whom she hands on her work when it is finished, is kept waiting; and the psychological effect of knowing that someone of your own sort is sitting waiting for you to finish (even if you also know that she doesn't mind waiting) provides an automatic, almost unconscious, incentive greater than any reprimand. In fact, so strong is this feeling that most people's ambition is to "have plenty in hand"—that is to say, get ahead of the next girl on the process, so that there is a pile waiting for her to do. This gives the comfortable sense of being able to slack off, without the irritating feeling of someone sitting and waiting for more.

A good deal of talk goes on during work in the Assembly. Conversation is much easier than in the machine shop, because there is less noise and we are sitting closer together—only two or three feet between each girl, whereas in the machine shop most of the machines were five or fix feet apart. Here are some selections from a typical morning's conversation on one of the benches. The speakers are:

Mary, F30C, unmarried, lives at home.
Phyllis, F35C, widow, with one little girl.
Poppy, F20C, unmarried, lives in billets.
Ellen, F20C, unmarried lives in billets.

MARY: Won't it be awful when they have the Utility clothes! They're going to be quite straight, my sister says, no pleats, no pockets, just straight down with a belt!

ELLEN: And the shoes! It would be awful to have Utility shoes. All the same, everyone you see all wearing the same! It cheers you up to have a bit of something different, doesn't it?

POPPY: Will they have the coupons for the Utility clothes just the same?

MARY: Oh, yes, there's coupons for everything. Everything of clothing.

POPPY: Yes, I know, I mean, will the coupons be the same amount? Like if you were buying a coat, would a Utility coat be as many coupons as an ordinary one?

MARY: Oh, I should think so. I should think it would be the same. Wouldn't you think so, Phyl.?

PHYLLIS: Eh?

MARY: Poppy was asking, would it be the same number of coupons to buy a Utility coat as an ordinary coat, and I said it would be the same. Don't you think it would be the same?

PHYLLIS: Oh, yes. They wouldn't make no difference to that. I mean, it's to save the material, that's why they're having them, isn't it?

Pause.

MARY: Do they have coupons for curtains?

ELLEN: No, my mother got some, and she didn't give up no coupons, I know she didn't.

PHYLLIS: When was that, Ellen? Because they've got them now. When was it you mean, how long ago?

ELLEN: Not long. Last summer.

PHYLLIS: Ah. Yes, you see, they've changed it. Curtains are on the coupons now. I know, because I got some in Swindon, but I had to give coupons. And I saw another woman in the shop, she was buying curtains too, but she had to give up her coupons. I saw her give them up,

Pause.

ELLEN: Did you hear that song on the wireless—"The White Cliffs of Dover"?

POPPY: I never listen to the wireless now, ours doesn't work any more. What is it?

ELLEN: It goes somehow like this (*begins to sing*): "And bluebirds are over"—You're laughing at me! You always laugh when I sing.

POPPY: I'm not! I'm trying to hear. I can't tell you if I can't hear what you're singing, can I?

ELLEN (*crossly*): You are, you're laughing at me. I've often seen you. You sit there laughing.

POPPY: If you knew what I was *really* laughing at, you'd think different. I don't trouble myself with other people's business.

ELLEN: Well, I don't see why you have to laugh when I sing. You're always singing yourself.

POPPY (*begins to sing softly*):

"Mary Ellen at the church turned up
Her Ma turned up and her Pa turned up
Her cousin Gert, and his Uncle Bert,
And the parson in his long white shirt
Turned up——"

How does it go next, Mary? You ought to know, it's a real old Lancashire song.

MARY: Something about the bridegroom never turned up . . .

POPPY: Yes, I know, but how does it go? I can't think . . .

MARY: But the bridegroom in his coach, he never turned up . . .

POPPY: That's right (*continues*):

"But the bridegroom in his coach he never turned up.
But a telegraph boy with his nose turned up
Brought a telegram to say that he couldn't come to-day
For they'd found him in the river with his toes turned up."

At this point, Joe, one of the inspectors on the bench, comes past:

"Cheerful this morning, aren't you?"

POPPY: Oh, yes, Joe, cheerful! We would be, Monday morning, wouldn't we? You're looking older this morning, Joe. Look at him, Phyl, he looks older, somehow, don't he?

JOE: Do I?

PHYLLIS: He always looks older than what he is, don't he? You're twenty-eight, aren't you, Joe? You'd never dream he was under thirty, not to look at him.

JOE: Ah, I've seen the shady side. That's why I look older.

POPPY: Have you, Joe? What have you seen?

JOE: Ah! *(goes away grinning)*.

ELLEN *looks up from the "Sketch", which she has been reading*: How do you pronounce M-Y-R-R-H?

PHYLLIS: How do you pronounce which? Let's have a look. Oh, Myrrh. Frankincense and myrrh. That's what the three wise men brought.

MARY: That's what they burn in the Catholic church. It makes you feel quite faint like. I was in a Catholic service once and they were burning incense, and I turned quite faint.

PHYLLIS: I haven't been to church once the last two years. Do you go to church much?

MARY: I haven't been since the war. I think you can be just as good a person, if you behave yourself decent—you know. Just as good as some of these church people, who go to church regular.

PHYLLIS: That's what I always say. Hypocrites, some of them are.

JOE *reappears, and starts some very noisy filing just beside Poppy's chair*:

POPPY: Joe! You're setting my teeth—Oh, it's awful! Oh, Joe, stop!

JOE: Can't be helped. Work's got to be done.

POPPY: Oh, Joe, stop! You don't have to. Why come up here to do it? Whenever you've got anything noisy to do you bring it up near me, just because you know I hate it. Why can't you do it down your own end?

JOE *grins, and continues filing.*

COMPLAINTS AND CRITICISMS

(a) *By newcomers from the machine shop.*

From the foregoing description it might be imagined that anyone coming from the machine shop would be thankful for the relief from boredom offered by this more interesting and constructive work. But it seems that to most of them this advantage is more than offset by the burden of responsibilities, which a year or more in the machine shop has ill fitted them to cope with. And undoubtedly, after being in the machine shop for even a short time and then coming out again, one does miss very much the sense of complete and utter freedom from cares and responsibilities of all kinds; the feeling of security and peace that comes from having every moment of the day, whether pleasant or otherwise, planned and arranged for by someone else. Many of the complaints heard from these girls refer to this new and unwelcome responsibility.

"I hate it here," says Lena. "I'm doing just the same work I was doing before, but I have to set it up as well as drill it. I don't like it. I don't think it's fair to make you set it up, and then tell you off if you've done it wrong."

And Eileen:

"If you want to have an evening off, they won't let you have it without you've finished your amount of work! Over the machine shop you only had to ask and he'd let you off, here they come quizzing round what you've done and what you haven't done, and if they aren't satisfied they won't let you go."

The change of times for breaks has also been a big grievance. In the machine shop the breaks were: ten minutes at ten a.m.; dinner from one to two p.m.; tea from six to six-thirty p.m. In the Assembly there is no break in the morning; dinner from twelve till one; a short tea break from three-twenty to three-thirty; and then a half-hour for tea from five-thirty to six. The girls from the machine shop can't get over the loss of the ten-minute break in the morning (which certainly did seem to make a great difference), and they also dislike coming back from tea at six instead of six-thirty; the two hours till eight seeming much longer than the hour and a half to which they have been accustomed. They forget that the long four-hour stretch in the afternoon, which they used to dread, has now been broken up. It seems that once psychologically adapted to one set of hours, any change feels like a change for the worse.

(b) *By permanent Assembly workers.*

The Assembly girls are more vocal in their grievances than were the machine shop girls. As in the machine shop, the most frequently and most bitterly discussed grievance is the length of the hours. But the Assembly girls are much quicker to suggest that they *ought* to be cut down—not merely to wish helplessly:

> "They've no right to keep us here these hours. I don't know any other factory that works like we do." (F30C)
>
> "I think it's silly. I don't believe they get a bit more work out of us than if they let us go half-past five. You get so tired, you can't work the same, it stands to reason." (F35C)
>
> "They ought to be made to cut them down. They will too. I saw in the paper they're going to put all the factories on shift work, eight hours a day, and no one will be allowed to work twelve hours like we do." (F25CD)

There is, too, a certain amount of thought-out criticism of mismanagement, with reference to other factors than mere personal likes and dislikes. A complaint of this sort heard several times was about the time-sheets; the time-sheets are small printed forms, about three inches by two inches, on which each girl has to fill in each day what job she is working on, and what time she started and finished. No one can make out quite what the point of this is, as *all* information is already on the clock-cards, but whereas in the machine-shop no one worried about it one way or the other, in the Assembly one heard remarks like this:

> "It's wicked the way they waste paper here. The way they make you start a new clocking card, if there's only two days used on your last one. And the time-sheets, that's a waste of paper. They never look at them, I know they don't. They

don't use them at all, those office girls. They just collect them up and never look at them. It's a wicked waste." (F35C)[1]

or this:

"What's it for, all these time-sheet things?"
"For the salvage, of course" (*general laugh*).

A frequent complaint from the girls who had been here for some time was about the room itself. As we have said, it is very large and lit all the time by artificial lights. Though the lighting is good from the physiological point of view, many of them felt bitterly never seeing the daylight:

"You sometimes think you'll go mad, summer time, shut up in here like night time, when the sun is shining away outside."

"I hate this place. If you could just see a bit of the sky out of the window even, it wouldn't be so bad."

"They say this light's very good for your eyes, but it can't be like daylight. It's not right to keep people shut in all day long like this."

Those who remember the old Assembly department, just a part of the original house itself, look back on it with longing:

"I don't like this new place. We used to be upstairs, it was so nice, like a real old mansion, you went up a lovely old polished staircase, and all the oak walls and everything, I used to look forward to coming in in the mornings, it was so pretty. You could have all the windows open, and you could look out on to the lawn, and there was a fountain and a goldfish pond, where this place is built now. We could see all the grass and the flowers in the sun, and all the lovely fresh air coming in in the summer. It seemed wicked to knock it all to pieces and put this thing up. We saw them doing it, and we thought it was wicked. It's all clammy down here, like being in prison, and you never see the sun any more.

[1] This lack of appreciation of a system which is not understood points to the issue of a small broadsheet describing functions of the various forms and systems, etc., in simple language, dealing with one section of the factory at a time. Actually the slip in question was the means whereby the Costing Department would know on which particular job the employee in question had been engaged for the day—(*Labour Manager*).

It was awful, we sat there watching them putting it up, and we knew that once it was finished we'd never see the sun any more.

"It's never been the same since, not the people, nor anything. It used to be all so friendly and nice, but I don't like it now. I don't like any of them." (F20C)

"I used to be very happy in the Assembly, but I'm browned off now. I don't like being inside like this; I sometimes feel if I don't get out I shall go balmy. Do you know, sometimes I have to think to myself, is it morning or afternoon now? You can't tell, can you, down here? You can't tell whether it's summer or winter or day or night. I don't like it." (F25C)

In this long hall of concentrated, skilful war-effort, there is a sort of everlasting simmer of minor discontent.[1]

7

ATTITUDE TO AUTHORITY

CHARGE-HANDS

(a) *In the Machine Shop.*

The charge-hands in the machine shop are all men, in their twenties and early thirties. One and all they pay much more attention to the mechanical side of their job—setting up and generally looking after apparatus and machinery—than to their other task of discipline and leadership among the girls on their bench. They almost all adopt the same attitude to the girls—one of amused tolerance; nothing a girl can do will bring her a reprimand from a charge-hand; the worst she has to fear is a piece of good-humoured sarcasm. The girls themselves revel in this situation. If the charge-hands choose to look on them with amused masculine superiority as scatterbrained little nitwits who can't do anything right, then what can be easier than to

[1] The Assembly Hall was actually built to Ministry specification; no windows were allowed larger than 3 sq. ft. and below a level of 9 ft. Such windows as there are are obscured by anti-shatter material, and while all this is in the interest of employee's safety, it is naturally galling to those who remember the previous surroundings. In a town this would not be noticed, but when it is known that there are trees and fields outside, it is objectionable but unfortunately unavoidable—(*Works Manager*).

accept this role and make it a cover for any and every kind of carelessness and laziness? For this attitude takes the last shreds of responsibility for their actions from the girls' shoulders, and gives the final touches to that carefree atmosphere which is the machine shop's chief attraction.

An illustration of this:

> "Lou! Look, Lou, it's stuck somehow."

Lou comes to inspect the machine:

> "You've put it in crooked, that's why. You in love or something?"

He puts it right for her.

> "Oh, thank you, Lou. Funny how this machine's always going funny on me, isn't it? It don't seem to like me."
>
> "Don't like you, eh? These machines don't like anybody who can't use them right. No mechanical sense, that's what the matter with you girls. No mechanical sense."

She goes away smiling.

Although there is not much respect for the authority of charge-hands—there is no "Look out—he's coming" atmosphere as there is in the case of the foreman—they are all well-liked, with one exception. It is interesting that this exception is the only one of the charge-hands who does not adopt the attitude described above; in fact he deliberately tries to avoid it. He says:

> "I don't try to make myself out superior, like some of them. I always treat all the girls as my equals—I'm not supposed to, but I do. I've always come in with the workers. I'm a worker myself, and not ashamed of it."

This does not go down nearly so well with the girls, who much prefer to be regarded as not responsible for their own actions:

> "Oh, that twerp. I don't like being under him."

The present charge-hands, whatever their effect on production, are certainly much more popular than the female charge-hand who used to be head—a lot of the girls consciously disliked working under a woman:

"I don't like the women. We used to have a woman here, and she was terrible. She couldn't take a joke, like these ones do. One day she came into the cloakroom when I was putting polish on my nails, and she says to me, 'This isn't a beauty parlour, you know.' I thought she was joking—you know—so I said, 'I've only got two more to do.' She went off without saying anything, and I didn't think any more about it; but do you know, she'd gone off and told Mr. E. (foreman at that time) and he didn't half tell me off. Said he'd suspend me the next day. It was mean, wasn't it, to go and tell on me like that. That's the trouble with the women, they are mean when they get into a position." (F25C)[1]

(b) *In the Assembly.*

The charge-hands here are mostly women; this is indeed one of the objections the machine-shop girls have to working in the Assembly:

"It's cleaner in there I know, but I don't like the charge-hands. They're always watching over you, and they come and tell you off if you're standing around." (F30D)

But the girls actually in the Assembly do not object nearly as much. Women charge-hands are undoubtedly stricter disciplinarians than the men, but the Assembly girls take a certain amount of dicipline for granted, in a way in which the machine-shop girls are unwilling to do. The Assembly girls, however, though they do not object to discipline as such, are very sensitive to the manner in which it is administered. There are two charge-hands here, Mrs. B. and Mrs. C., who are both equally strict, as far as actual things they forbid and allow are concerned, but their manner of putting it across differs very much, as does their popularity with the girls. Mrs. B. is a youngish blonde woman, with a gentle, rather childlike voice, who always looks tired and harassed. She enforces her demands by a sort

[1] The supervision in this Shop has of necessity been recruited from the best elements in the rank and file. Naturally they lack supervisory training and in default thereof the Management are endeavouring to guide promoted supervisory grades in the technique of supervision. The expansion of War industry has made supervisory grades in all industries the rarest of the rare—(*Works Manager*).

of unassuming appeal which seems much more effective than direct firmness. The girls like her, and make an effort to see that nothing they do will get her into trouble:

"I'd go on with my knitting, but Mr. E. (the foreman) is snooping round this evening. I don't mind him, but if he sees me he'll tell Mrs. B. off." (F20C)

"She's ever so nice, she never tells you off if you don't finish. But I like to finish if I can, because she gets the blame in the end if this bench is slower than the rest." (F35C)

"I like our charge-hand. Sometimes I feel I want to kiss her when she's so nice—she speaks to you so politely, and no bullying. There's no 'Do this' and 'Do that' about her; it's always 'please' and 'Will you'?" (F25C)

Mrs. C., on the other hand, while in fact she enforces almost exactly the same degree of discipline, always seems to be enforcing a more stringent code, as these remarks about her show:

"She's a terror—always hanging round—'Don't do this'—'Don't do that'." (F20C)

"You always feel you mustn't even talk if she's around. Of course she can't stop you talking, not if you're getting on the same time, but you feel like that." (F30C-D)

"She'll never say 'Will you do so and so?' but always 'Why haven't you done it?' It's the same if she's showing you how to do anything—she seems to think you ought to know, as if she was telling you off for not knowing." (F30C)

"I don't like her. You feel all on the jump when she's around." (F30D)

Many of the charge-hands here fail to realise the immense importance which the girls attach to finding out *who's fault* a given mistake is. A busy charge-hand is naturally apt to feel that if some mistake occurs which either of two girls may be equally to blame for, the quickest and easiest solution is to tell them both indiscriminately that it mustn't happen again. But this method invariably rouses such a psychological storm that it is certainly not the best way, and probably not the quickest either. The following incident illustrates this point.

The screws on a certain piece of work were found by Inspection to have been screwed up too tight. This might have been the fault of the girl who originally had to put them in, Mary;

or it might be the fault of Rose, who later on had to unscrew them to do her own job, and then screw them up again the way she found them. When it was found that they arrived in Inspection done up too tight, the charge-hand took the apparently simple course of telling both girls just how tight to do them. But this aroused a storm of protest:

> "They were all right when I sent them up; she must have done them when she tightened them up again."
>
> "I didn't; I did them up just the way they came to me."
>
> "You couldn't have done. Miss J., I've been on this for months, and no one's complained before. . . ."
>
> "Well, all I know is, I did them up just the way they came to me. . . ."
>
> "I don't care who did it," the charge-hand breaks in. "All I care is, it isn't done again. You can fight it out for yourselves who's fault it is."

She could hardly have said anything more tactless. The result was half a morning spent on more and more heated wrangling, until at last a foreman had to intervene and sort out the rights and wrongs of the case in all their detail.

It is hard to suggest the proper solution to this sort of thing. Clearly, unlimited time can't be spent on assessing rights and wrongs, but on the other hand, if the authorities leave the (to them irrelevant) question of blame in mid-air, the girl who's fault it isn't (and practically always she knows in her heart whether it is her fault or not) is left with a quite disproportionate sense of grievance, which lasts for days and even weeks. One of the secrets of Mrs. B.'s popularity is that she always takes trouble to sift matters of this sort—even if she doesn't come to any conclusion, she gives the girl the feeling that she is being listened to, which is what she chiefly wants.

This problem is the more worth considering, as it is the girls who take a certain amount of pride and interest in their work who are most sensitive to implied or imagined slights on it.[1]

[1] This is very encouraging and shows interest where interest is wanted. It is obviously tied up, too, with the relationship between Charge-Hands and the workers, in this case as stated, recruited from the ranks. We have had much mores uccess in upgrading in this department than in, say, the Machine Shop, chiefly on account of the fact that there are five times the number of people and hence the choice is wider—(*Works Manager*).

FOREMEN

The present foreman in the machine shop is almost universally popular. He manages to combine effective authority with the same air of tolerant amusement that makes the chargehands here popular:

"He's very nice, the foreman here. He never tells you off; if you do something wrong, he kinds of jokes with you about it. He's awfully nice." (F25D)

"Mr. B. is very nice. He may look awful, but you know, he always makes a joke at the end." (F30D)

"He asked me why I wanted to go early, and I told him I'd got a lot to do. So he asked me, how are you going to get home all that way if you wait for the bus? So I told him that the parson goes past in his car and would pick us up. He knew it was a lie, he laughed and laughed. 'Good luck,' he said. He knew we were going to wave for a lift, I know he did, he laughed so." (F20C)

In the Assembly, the foremen are for the most part much less well known, and hardly at all talked about. Mr. B. in the machine shop is well known to everyone, and makes his personality felt. In the Assembly there are a number of girls who barely know who their foreman is; and apart from an occasional "Look out, he's coming!" the foremen are rarely mentioned or talked of. Their authority is recognised in a very impersonal way.

MANAGEMENT

In spite of their irresponsible and carefree outlook, the machine-shop girls have a quite surprising degree of regard for the really high-ups—a regard which might be taken much more advantage of than it is. When, as sometimes happens, the manager and some of his immediate circle come round the machine shop, there is usually a buzz of excited talk about it afterwards:

"He stopped for a long time to look at my machine. I thought he was going to speak to me."

"He stopped and spoke to me last time he came round. 'How are you getting on?' he asked me."

"He's very nice, the way he speaks to you, isn't he? Some managers, you might be one of the machines yourself. But he's not like that."

"That's the difference, you see. He knows his position and so he's polite to you. Some of them are scared for their position, and so they treat you like dirt."

"I think he's got ever such a nice kind face. I've never spoken to him."

"Does he know us all, do you think? Would he know my name?"

"He seems to know you, doesn't he? He sort of looks as if he knew you."

And there follows a lot of eager talk about occasions when he has and has not addressed various girls by name.

The only recorded occasion when there was any spontaneous talk in the machine shop about working harder, was one day when it was rumoured that the manager was going to make a speech congratulating the machine shop on their output:

"Oh, I do hope he will. I don't feel so fed up now."

"I'll finish my thousand before then."

"I suppose he knows how much we all do."

"He made a lovely speech last time, didn't he? I didn't mind that evening at all, I thought to myself, well, what a lot I'm doing!"

"He speaks lovely, doesn't he? He must have had a good education."

All this suggests that girls of the machine-shop type are far more influenced by a personality than they are by any number of abstract appeals to patriotism, or by impersonal regulations and penalties.[1]

In the Assembly the attitude is quite different. They have something of the more sophisticated worker-versus-boss attitude, and are critical of the whole management in a way one never meets in the machine shop. The figure of the manager

[1]This should be made more use of—(*Labour Manager*).

Agreed. Every three months it is my intention to make a statement to the workers in person. General complaints will be put straight from the shoulder and praise distributed where and when earned. This personal aspect has definitely been under-rated but is rather a difficult problem. It will be discussed later—(*Works Manager*).

still forms the focal point of all talk about the management, and here a lot of the talk about him is very critical:

"I've never known him give a lift to anyone. Often I've seen him drive through the town, and somebody may be going along, missed the bus or something, and he's all alone in that great car, he never picks them up. People would think a lot more of him if he did a thing like that. But he's not that sort. He just wants to be fat and comfortable. He's a Jew, you see." (F20C)

"All he thinks of is the money he can get out of us. He doesn't consider his workers." (F25D)

Some criticise him for being snobbish:

"He goes about in that great red car and thinks himself too good to look at anybody." (F35C)

Others for not being snobbish enough:

"He comes from Manchester, and he talks like this: (*imitates north country accent*). You'd have thought he'd have tried to pull himself up to it, wouldn't you, when he found he was manager, but he's let himself stay right down low. I don't think a manager of a big factory should be like that; he ought to think of his position.

"He isn't very smart, is he, but I suppose she takes all his clothes coupons." (F20D)

But even here, a straight appeal from the boss himself, when it is delivered in a personal sort of way, has an almost magical effect. A short time ago the manager made a speech in which he had to put across some really very unpalatable news about pay; namely, that pay day was to be shifted from Tuesday to Friday, so that on a coming week, one would virtually lose three days' pay—to get it back only at that fairy tale time "After the war". Before the speech it was rumoured that this was what he was going to say, and there was a lot of aggrieved talk about it; that it was not fair; we should never get it back, and so on. But afterwards, there was nothing but praise for the speech and its subject matter:

"He was very good. He must have an insight. He thought of all the points people are troubling about." (F35C)

"I liked him. I real liked him. I never thought I should, but I did." (F25D)

"He was very good, wasn't he. And he was quite right, too." (F30C)

"I'd never have thought to look at him that he'd speak so well." (F20C)

"Oh, he does sometimes. He makes lovely speeches. It was very fair, I think, the way he put it about the money, you can borrow it back for twelve weeks. I thought it was very fair, that, as if he'd thought about it, you know—thought what would be best for the workers." (F25C)

(The last two girls were among the loudest to complain about the project *before* the speech.)

Knowledge of, and interest in other members of the staff is slight, though rather greater than in the machine shop. There is a good deal of rather rambling complaint about "them"; but the "them" does not refer exactly to the staff; it refers to a sort of hazy mixture of office girls, Mr. Bevin, a lot of typed notices, and a row of people who sit at the far end of the canteen. They don't really distinguish very much between one member and another, apart from the manager, and, to a lesser degree, the Labour Manager, whom they all see when they first arrive. They take no sides, and have practically no knowledge of the skirmishings and squabblings that go on up top. They are as if at the peaceful bottom of the sea, which feels no ripple of the storms and tempests that may be going on about the surface.

The fact that the figure of the manager dominates in the girls' minds suggests that there is much more scope for personal leadership in a factory of this sort than is generally supposed. It is true that two hundred years of struggle between workers and management have done much to make such leadership by a manager difficult; but the foundations for it must be there, for these girls who have no industrial background, and so have little awareness of this tradition of struggle, take readily and spontaneously to the idea of leadership by the boss.[1]

[1]All this merely points to the well-known fact that subjective thinking is the order of the day. Evidently those who are attracted to me personally are attracted by those very factors which cause others to dislike me. If you give lifts in your car you are favouring; if you don't you are a snob. Some managers make a definite point of going right out to "sell" themselves to their employees, hoping by their personal popularity to get over many of the difficulties of management. This does not appeal to all managements, however, and the danger is that it is bound to lead to subjective thinking on

NOTICES PUT UP BY THE MANAGEMENT

In every work room there is a notice board on which numbers of typed notices are put up about any changes or events that are to take place, or any other subject of general interest to the factory. Among these are a number of would-be stimulating notices, exhorting workers to make more effort. Some of these are simply copies of articles in the press about e.g. how hard they work in Russian factories; these are too long to be read by a large proportion of girls. Others are definitely threatening and ill-natured in tone—spiteful little cuttings from the papers about how some worker was fined £10 for being late for work or how some girl was compelled to return to her job when she left it without permission. Whatever the intention of these notices, the effect they have is deplorable—that is, on the comparatively small number of girls who read them at all; they have definitely lowered the popularity of the management, especially the Welfare Manager:

> "I used to think a lot of Mr. G. (Welfare Manager), but I don't now, and I'll tell you why. All those notices about restrictions, and all the awful things they are going to do to us, they're all signed by him. I used to think he was the sort who'd stand up for us, but he doesn't seem to be, by the look of those." (F20C)
>
> "I'm not interested in this place any more. All they seem to do is look through the papers to find how they can punish us for what we haven't done yet. You can just see them sitting there with a pair of scissors and gloating when they find a bit to cut out and scare us with." (F30C)

A short time ago a notice in this sort of tone was sent round, saying that anyone who was more than five minutes late would

---

the part of managements themselves. The cure would then be worse than the evil. In my opinion the correct line is to be just, approachable, but not unduly familiar. Avoid cheapening oneself at all costs, and use every opportunity to impress on those who are responsible to you, your sincerity and desire to get on with the job.

All action should tend towards educating workers to objective thinking and the assumption of responsibility for their actions. This of course tends to be very difficult as there is invariably a large mass of executives interposed between the manager and the workers, and executives do not always think or act on the same lines as managements. The process therefore is of necessity slow, and full of discouragement; it is part and parcel of the job of managing a War factory—(*Works Manager*).

be reported to the National Service Officer. This was the reaction of some Assembly girls:

"That twerp again! Can't stop writing, can he?"

"Another bit of waste paper."

"What will he do to you—the National Service Officer?"

"Hang you up and leave you to die slowly, I should think!"

"Why don't they put us all in prison and have done with it?"

"They'd like to, wouldn't they. You can tell that, the way they put it."

"They keep on, don't they. Just as if we didn't know we were caught here. They can do what they like, and they know it."

8

FACTORY AMENITIES

(i) FOOD

Food and meal times occupy a good deal of attention, and the girls eat a noticeably large amount, considering the inactive nature of their work. For instance, a girl working in the machine shop usually has a hot breakfast before she leaves home in the morning; at ten o'clock she has tea and cheese rolls; at one o'clock there is dinner—meat and vegetables and pudding; at six she has high tea (cheese pie, or fish cakes, or something like that) and then usually a hot supper, when she gets back in the evening. And in addition to this, most of them bring cakes and sandwiches to eat at odd times during the morning—or more often during the four-hour stretch in the afternoon.

There seems to be a definite relation between boredom and this large consumption of food. Eating makes a change and relief from monotony as nothing else does. Even if one is not hungry, it is a great relief during the long afternoon to have a piece of cake, to look forward to; to be able to say to oneself: At four o'clock I'm going to stop and eat my cake. It makes a sort of landmark to look forward to and plan about, which is difficult with all other kinds of slacking, most of which just happen without the possibility of plan. And at break times, going up to the canteen makes much more of a change than just staying in the work room; and once you are up in the canteen the obvious thing to do is to have something to eat or drink.

The canteen is a large, airy room, furnished with a dozen or so very long wooden tables, and folding chairs. Food is served from the counter at one end, and the moment the buzzer goes, a long queue forms in front of the counter, waiting to be served. The food itself is excellent, and the menus have clearly been carefully planned by someone with a good knowledge of food values. For instance, when there is no meat or other protein food, beans are always the main vegetable. It is usually hot and, considering the difficulties, quickly served; and it is no easy matter for half a dozen or so girls to serve two hundred people in a space of ten or fifteen minutes (which is what they usually manage it in) even from a counter.

Though the quality of the food is, on the whole, fairly well appreciated, there are also a number of vigorous complainers. The complaints are not usually very specific, but embrace the whole of the canteen food, staff, and organisation in one breath. Condemnation, when expressed at all, tends to be complete:

> "I wouldn't touch the muck they give you up there for anything." (F35C)
>
> "I couldn't eat the canteen dinners. I wonder the girls aren't all poisoned, eating that stuff every day." (F20C)
>
> "If you had to live on what they give you here, you'd starve." (F20D)
>
> "If you can stand the food there for a fortnight, then your digestion will stand anything." (M30C)
>
> "It's disgusting. The food's enough to make you sick to look at it, and the prices are a robbery. I wouldn't like to make pigs in a sty eat the way we do. Sometimes I have to take my cup back four times before I get a clean one. Bits of egg between the prongs of your fork. That sort of thing. And those dirty little sluts of waitresses, all of them ought to be taken and put in a licebath!" (M30C)
>
> "The stuff they give you there is only fit for the pig-bucket." (F20C)

The fact that the complaints heard are in the main so sweeping and so obviously emotive in tone, leads one to suspect at once that their basis is psychological rather than material. From this standpoint, there seem to be three main factors at work.

The first appears most strongly in people who are resenting the whole fact of being in the factory at all. Their unwillingness to come here and their dislike of the work leads them to dislike indiscriminately anything to do with the factory life; and they vent this feeling on any aspect of the life which it is in their power to reject; food is one of the few things there which comes into this category.

The second factor is simple snobbishness, and appears much more among women than among men. Girls who are pretending (to themselves quite as much as to anyone else) that they have come from more prosperous homes than they have, tend to hammer in this impression by belittling the food they get away from home in comparison with the food they get at home. By turning up her nose at a steak and kidney pie provided by the canteen, a girl feels she is paying a tribute to the steak and kidney pies she is accustomed to at home. This has always been a common symptom among girls having meals at work.

These two types of attitudes are both found most commonly among girls of the C and upper D classes (the B's are mostly very appreciative of canteen food). The third attitude, which in a sense is a more genuine one, is found among lower D's. The reason for objection here is that they are genuinely unaccustomed to that type of food. A woman who is accustomed to making her dinner off a couple of slices of bread-and-margarine with a taste of pickles or German sausage, does not know quite what to make of a plate of steamed fish with a strange sauce over it, and some dark-coloured beans that she has never seen before in her life. The line of least resistance when confronted by this apparition, is to call it "muck", and bring sandwiches filled with familiar sixpenny brawn.

Of genuine complaints about specific material points there are few. Indeed, there is not really very much room for complaint, because nowhere in the country could one get a better meal at a lower price just now; a good helping of roast meat and vegetables, followed by pudding, for under a shilling, for instance. The only two specific complaints at all frequently heard, are that the washing-up is not good enough, and (rather vaguely) that people push into the front of the queue out of turn. As indeed they do, but it is difficult to know how to prevent this, except by force of public opinion.

And of course there are a number of minor and purely individual complaints based on personal likes and dislikes—"The meat's overdone", "The meat's underdone", "I don't like rice pudding", and so on.

Apart from the washing-up, there is very little to be altered in the canteen with any advantage. For the bulk of the complaints are based on a psychological situation with which it is no part of a cook's business to cope.[1]

(ii) THE ENSA CONCERTS

These take place every Thursday afternoon during the tea break. They consist of a short variety programme by touring artists, and vary very much in nature and quality from week to week. To make any isolated study of items liked and disliked is out of the question, as much more depends on the complicated factors of personality and method of putting it across than on anything that could be illustrated. Therefore a few very general observations will have to suffice.

The concerts were definitely looked forward to with considerable zest—perhaps more as a landmark in the week than for themselves:

> "I don't feel so bad now that Tuesday's nearly over. To-morrow I'm going off early, and then on Thursday there's the Ensa, and after that it's almost the week-end." (F20D)
>
> "I'm going to go off early Friday. I might have gone Thursday, but it's a pity to go the concert night. It makes a bit of a break." (F25C)

But there was too a certain amount of eagerness for the concert itself. There was a more frantic rush than usual to get

[1] This aspect of the psychological problem is naturally at the root of a good deal of managerial headache—it arises from the "we" and "they" attitude. Anything "they" do tends to be criticised as a matter of course, and as the Canteen is one of the things that "they" provide, it is a fair subject for adverse comment.

As a matter of interest the factory produces within its own grounds, all its own vegetables, and in addition runs a pig farm. Lettuce and tomatoes are available at normal charges out of season, and boiled hams cured locally, are quite a regular feature. For many months salads simply could not be sold, but as a result of Ministry of Food propaganda and persistence, they are now extremely popular. (This is unusual according to analysis of working class diet.) Only last week complaints were actually heard about a charge of 6d. per plate for a round of ham and a large lettuce salad. An Englishman is the most conservative eater in the world and the working classes are by far the most conservative part of the nation.

At a recent Works Committee Meeting I complained bitterly of petty complaints about the food, and one answer from a workers' representative was, "Well, people must have something to grumble about, and next to weather, food is the most universal target. It's just a safety valve like the speakers in Hyde Park"—(*Works Manager*).

up to the canteen and grab a place the moment the buzzer went, and afterwards there was always a lot of interested talk and criticism. It was clear from this talk that most of the girls were more interested in the performers as persons than they were in the actual show. Most of the talk was of this sort:

"I liked the little blondie, I thought she had a sweet little face. That accordion was too heavy for her, didn't you think? I liked the way she did her hair, too, it was very sweet." (F30D)

"Didn't you like her dress—that dark girl? I liked that snake on the front. I thought it was ever so smart." (F20D)

"I didn't like that man, he made himself look so silly somehow. I didn't like his great red face." (F20D)

"Didn't she have a lovely ring on her finger? I saw it flashing right across the room. I rather like the man's face too. He was like one of my uncles, sort of kind looking." (F20C)

"I didn't like that woman at the piano. She looked so stuck up and superior. A proper snob she looked." (F25C)

"I thought he was very attractive. He didn't have a strong voice, but it was a nice voice. He had a nice lean face—the artistic type." (F20C)

"I thought those two girls were nice. They weren't pretty, but they were the sort you'd notice coming down the street. You'd look at them twice." (F20C)

(Note: All these remarks are by C or D class girls. The reactions of B class we had little opportunity of studying, but it appeared to be a good deal less favourable.)

The machine-shop girls have a reputation for bad behaviour during these concerts:

"Those machine-shop girls have been spoiling it again, Maurice said. The man was going all red, he told me—they were setting on him. You know—those cat-calls the way they do. I think those girls are disgusting." (F20C, Assembly)

Actually the machine shop girls enjoy the concerts as much as anyone, and their comments afterwards are always more favourable than anyone else's. A large part of their reputation for bad manners at the concerts is due to their habit of showing their appreciation of a performer by loud conversations about his good qualities while the show is still going on.[1]

[1] The Workers' Committee has actually complained about the low quality of the humour in many Ensa Concerts, and requested more music and straight

(iii) TRANSPORT

A large proportion of the workers come from outlying districts, many of them fifteen miles away or more. A factory 'bus service was therefore imperative, and has now become an established institution.

From the girls themselves we heard practically no complaints (or indeed comments of any kind) about the 'bus service. Nevertheless there seems to have come to the ears of the management a demand for a 'bus to and from the town—a distance of about a mile. Some time ago they tried to satisfy this demand by making the long distance buses collect their own passengers first and deposit them at the factory, and then go into the town and collect people from there—completing the whole thing by eight a.m. Similarly in the evening the town workers were taken home first, and then the buses went on their more distant destinations. But this was soon given up, because it meant that those who lived a long way off, and already had barely ten hours for leisure, food and sleep, had their free time docked by yet another half hour, while the local girls who were already better off in this respect, had the situation changed even more in their favour.

Whether at this time there was a big demand for such a bus or not we cannot say from first-hand experience. But certainly from the time of study (at the beginning of February), we heard next to nothing about buses at all. And this covered a period which included a considerable amount of snow and sleet and bitter winds, when any complaints there might be would be expected to be at their height. The only definite complaint heard from the local girls in the machine shop was when buses from the outlying districts were prevented from running by bad weather. They objected that it was unfair that they had to come in and work while the rest stayed comfortably at home because of buses. They also regret that they have not the perfect and unanswerable excuse: "I missed the bus" which others use for their stolen days off.

---

stuff. Two C.E.M.A. Concerts (classical, instrumental and vocal music) have been very successful, and attempts have been made for more, as well as for lunch-time gramophone recitals, which it is hoped to start very shortly. These demands emanate from a small but important section of the more skilled employees—(*Works Manager*).

(iv) MONEY

The basic material circumstance, earnings, is in general fairly favourable to the worker. The majority of employees are young girls without much previous industrial experience or skill, and without serious economic responsibility. The wages average about £2 14*s*., and many get a lot more. Spending outlets in this district are very restricted; they are considered in Chapter 10 (especially pp. 92–96). The weaknesses here of a purely Cash Incentive are discussed in Chapter 13 (pp. 119–120).

This brief survey of the main amenities of the factory shows that the Management has a fair standard of effort in the direction of material welfare, and a very creditable degree of achievement in comfort facilities. The shortcomings of life here which we have discussed, and will discuss in coming pages, are not primarily the outcome of neglect in purely materialistic directions.

SECTION III

LEISURE

9

SOCIAL LIFE IN WAR VILLAGE

"THERE'S NOTHING TO do in this dump."

This is a phrase one hears over and over again, from soldiers, from factory workers, from Air Ministry employees—from everyone, in fact, who has been brought in to the village, more or less involuntarily, for the duration of the war. And a walk through the town on Sunday afternoon will, superficially, lend weight to this complaint. At every corner there are knots of soldiers, just standing. Some are smoking, some not even doing that; others are strolling languidly up and down outside the Y.M.C.A. Though they are less in evidence, the situation is much the same with the girl workers. Some of them are to be seen wandering about the streets in twos or threes, aimlessly, and in no special direction; but an even greater number are still sitting in their billets, with no household jobs to occupy them, idling over a piece of mending, or writing a letter. And the reason given for all this lack of definite occupation is the same—"There's nothing to do."

Now, to some extent this is the natural reaction of the town dweller to sudden transportation to a country place; he takes a long time to adapt himself to the idea of providing his own amusements instead of finding them ready-made. But in this case there is something more. The trouble here is that a very big proportion of this imported population has no intention of adapting itself. They know they are there only temporarily; they know that, after a shorter or longer space of time, they will leave this place and never see it again. There is thus an overpowering atmosphere of "it's not worth bothering" which hangs like a pall over any attempt to organise social activities of any kind, other than standard entertainments like cinemas and dances, to which one can go mechanically and from habit, without any mental or emotional effort.

These, then, are the only two kinds of social activity for which there is anything approaching a popular demand; and of these, it is only the cinema that is really well attended.[1]

THE CINEMA

There is only one cinema in the town, and it quite small. The show is changed twice a week, and on Sunday evenings there is a special programme put on by the factory authorities themselves.[2] There is always a long queue for every showing during the weekend, particularly on Saturday evenings. There is some resentment of this among the natives:

> "We didn't ought to have to wait like this. They ought to let us get in first, we've lived here all our lives, and let the others wait. Pushing in front like they do, and I don't suppose they knew there was such a place as —— six weeks ago." (F40D)

The pictures is the one event in the week which the factory girls really do look forward to and enjoy. There is always a lot of talk about films as the weekend approaches, and going forms a sort of focal point to an otherwise aimless and drifting weekend. There are few complaints from them about the queueing, which some of them seem quite to enjoy:

> "Let's get there real early tonight, and see who's there. We could get some fish and chips and stand there and eat them while they're all hot and nice. You can't really eat them when you're pushing in, can you?" (F20C)

[1] This is a very fair summing up. Townsfolk naturally tend towards ready-made amusements, i.e. watching football matches, going to the cinema, etc. To such an extent does the town dweller have his amusement "served up on a plate" that he is quite lost without the usual amenities. The country dweller, on the other hand, used to make his own arrangements, but now in the country too, amusement has to be served on a platter, and there is very little attempt on the part of people to provide their own entertainment, hence the success of the cinema.

Recently, however, a most successful Sports' Day was held in a nearby park, and it was a tremendous success. The percentage of persons entering the actual events was very high—(*Works Manager*).

[2] Actually the Sunday evening cinema was started by an enthusiastic nucleus of the members of the Works Social and Sports Club, who arranged to hire the cinema for the evening in question, and seats are bookable at the Works during the week. Prior to the "industrial invasion" there was no attempt to provide a Sunday cinema. As a means of creating goodwill, seats not actually booked in advance are available to H.M. Forces and then to all comers—(*Works Manager*).

DANCES

There is quite a big selection of available dances. The Catholic School (which has a good-sized hall) holds dances on Mondays, Thursdays and Saturdays; the Social Centre on Saturdays and Sundays; and the intervening days are frequently filled up by odd dances, held by the R.A.M.C., or by some other section of the local Forces. The average price of entrance at these dances is 1*s*.

Most of them are fairly well attended, but not very lively affairs. There are usually many more girls than men, and the men who are there tend to hang about in corners and not dance; many of them have come simply for the universal reason—"There's nothing to do." By about ten things usually begin to warm up a bit, but even then there is not the atmosphere of real, wholehearted enjoyment that one usually gets at working-class dances. One of the organisers of the Catholic School dances (M25C) said:

> "You know, at the end of the evening I feel—I can't describe it. As if I'd been pushing heavy weights about for hours. I don't know what's the matter with people down here—you can't put any life in them."[1]

The reason for this is, of course, that so many of them have come simply because they can think of nothing better to do. They haven't even any very strong desire to make friends—one of the most usual reasons for going to dances—because so many of them feel that they are here for only a short time; they have all the friends they want at home, and all their interests are focused on counting the days till the next weekend, when they can go there.

THE SOCIAL CENTRE

Nowhere is this attitude shown more clearly than by the poor attendance at most of the functions here. The Centre was started by the factory authorities some months ago, with Government backing, as they felt that newcomers to the town would want somewhere to spend their evenings and make friends. It is ideally situated in the centre of the town, and contains a small hall which can be used for dancing; a bar; and several smaller

[1] See note in Appendix on "cottonwoolliness"—(*Works Manager*).

rooms which can be used as reading rooms, lecture rooms, and so on. The subscription is 15*s.* a year, (or 1*s.* 6*d.* a month), and membership is open to anyone, in or out of the factory.

It caters primarily, of course, for newcomers to the town, and the idea was basically an excellent one. But the authorities did not take into account (indeed, it would have been hard to foretell it beforehand) the aloof and disinterested attitude which so many newcomers were going to adopt to their whole life here. Instead of settling down to build up a new life and circle of friends here, workers pushed into the town by circumstances or force, have firmly maintained all their home interests and friends; their home is still the only real life to them, and the sojourn here merely an irritating or distressing interlude, to be got through as quickly as possible. A number of remarks made about the Social Centre illustrate, directly and indirectly, this attitude:

> "I wouldn't trouble myself to go there. I don't care about the —— girls, and I wouldn't trouble myself to trail round there just on the chance of making friends." (F20C)
>
> "I think it's very nice, what I've heard of it, and if I was really living here I'd expect I go. But I can get home most weekends, so it wouldn't be worth my while joining." (F25C)
>
> "They only go there to try and find a young man, most of them. I've got my young man up in Yorkshire, I don't want to go hunting round for no more." (F25D)
>
> "I don't know, I'm not very interested. I'm not very interested in this place at all." (F25C)

This attitude towards social life of any kind here, is a fundamental one, and I can think of no changes in the organisation or programme of the Social Centre which could have any effect on it at all. Far deeper and more radical changes in the whole structure of wartime life would be needed, quite outside the scope of any single locality or organisation.

It is interesting, however, to consider a few minor points in this social centre which detract from its popularity.

In the first place, the fact that it is organised and sponsored by the factory authorities and that they are often to be found there, is one which cannot be forgotten. Many of the lower-grade employees feel as shy of meeting any of their bosses "out of school" as are school-children of meeting their masters and mistresses. A lot of the reasons for not joining seem to hinge on this:

"The Social Club? Isn't that where Mr. G. (Welfare Manager) and all of them go? I wouldn't like to go in there." (F25D)

"I'd be scared. I'd be scared I'd meet Mr. L. (Manager) there." (F20D)[1]

Closely allied to this, is the feeling among many, e.g. the machine-shop employees, that it is the exclusive preserve of the office staff:

"Oh no. I don't belong. It's for the office girls really." (F30D)

"Well, you have to be a bit posh to go there, don't you." (F20D)

"I wouldn't go in there, with all them snobs from the office. I'd rather go to an ordinary dance." (F20D)

And in fact, it is mainly office staff and higher grade employees who go there, although this is quite contrary to the original founders' idea of the place.

Another thing is that the small number of people who do habitually go there have got to know each other so well that any newcomer tends to feel rather out of it:

"I've been round there two or three times, but they're funny there. So stand-offish. I poked my nose in there on Saturday night, but I soon brought it out again. They were all sitting round the walls whispering, and nobody spoke to me. It was miserable." (F25C)

"They're all such a clique there, all in together." (F25I)

"I don't like going in there. I've only been once or twice, and they look at you as if they wonder why you are there." (F20D)

"*That's* what I don't like about that place. Last time I went there they were all sitting round the fire all close together. I couldn't see a bit of the fire, and nobody asked me if I'd like to have a look at it too." (F25D)

"I can't go. I don't know anybody." (F20D)[2]

[1] I think it advisable that Management representatives should drop out of Social Centre activities as quickly as possible—(*Labour Manager*).

Agreed, as soon as the rank and file are able and willing to take over—(*Works Manager*).

[2] Obviously more drive is needed to get employees into the Social Centre. Possibly the Management can subsidise a month's temporary membership for new employees—(*Labour Manager*).

A good idea. Why not offer a month's membership on approval? Suggest this to the Committee—(*Works Manager*).

These, then, are about the sum total of social activities here. Attempts to organise anything further—like dramatic groups, cycling or walking clubs, and so on—all at their very outset run up against the same barrier—lack of lively demand for such activities, due to total lack of interest in the village as a social unit.[1]

In the next three chapters will be shown in detail the way leisure time actually is spent by girls living at home, by those in billets, and by those at the hostel.

10

AT HOME

THE FAMILY GROUP

> "Do you know, I sometimes envy these girls in billets? I know it's miserable, for them never getting back to see their people and that, but I sometimes think I'd rather that than the way I live. I'm living at home, I know, but it doesn't feel like it. I get back just when they're all going to bed, and I go away in the morning without seeing only Mum. I might just as well be living in lodgings, really I might."

This is a more than usually explicit statement of a feeling that a number of girls are beginning to have; a feeling that they are being more and more cut off from family life—that while the skeleton of it is still theirs, the substance of it is gone. All the day-to-day family occurrences in which they would normally be sharing happen in their absence; all the people who may call have gone before they get back; even the family meals are all over, and a special plate of something is produced for them to eat on their own. As one girl living in a nearby town put it, half laughing and half bitter:

[1] On a number of occasions a well-organised show has been put on. A few people have worked really hard to plan an evening's entertainment. These have been very successful, but unfortunately the lack of push and ambition, which is a by-product of our social conditions, makes the average rank and file worker shy of coming forward and taking a leading part. There is a natural tendency every time that a new committee is being elected for those persons to put themselves forward who also put themselves forward in other walks of life, i.e. in their everyday work; in fact the problems of leadership and responsibility at the Club boil down to the same problems as at work. It is part of the "we" and "they" complex referred to previously. It is all left to "they" to organise, leaving the "we" to criticise but not take part —(*Labour Manager*).

"I get back nine o'clock, and they've got the wireless on, and Dad's asleep in the chair, and the kiddies are in bed, and Mum's so sleepy she don't know whether she's on her head or her heels—and I don't blame her, poor old soul, she's up half-past five every morning. I tell her sometimes, I tell her: 'Mum, you'll have to be writing me letters every week to tell me what goes on in this house.' I feel like that you know—as if I was away. Do you know, I haven't seen Johnny (her little brother) for two weeks now—only when he's asleep."

And another:

"We used to have the girls come in after tea every evening almost, me and my sister. Ever such fun we used to have, but they never come now, hardly. I don't get back till nearly nine, and they have gone out somewhere. I don't like to go on by myself—you know, walk in late to things. I wouldn't like it, not on my own like that."

Sometimes this segregation from the ordinary family life makes the girl feel almost an intruder in her home. One girl of about eighteen described rather bitterly an occasion which had made her feel like this:

"The billeting officer had been round, and they were talking about it when I got in. 'What's happening?' I asked; 'Are we to have some evacuees? I hope it's not children. Don't let them send us any children, Mum, we've enough of children in this house.' Quite nicely I said it, but Doreen (her sister) turned on me quite sharp. 'You leave it to Mum and me,' she said; 'it don't matter to you who we have and who we don't, you're never there.' Just as if it wasn't my home as much as hers. I told her, it was a nasty thing to say, I didn't expect my own sister to say a thing like that, I told her."

The attitude is not usually so conscious and outspoken as this; but nevertheless it is there in embryo in many homes. It is all part of the shifting and unstable background in which these girls' lives are now framed; and it is in the light of this background that we must now go on to consider their leisure interests and activities.

WEEKDAY EVENINGS

Queries about ways of spending the evening usually receive answers like these:

> "I get home at nine o'clock, and I go straight to bed. I've no time even to do any mending. I don't like to put it on Mother, but I can't help it. I just haven't time." (F25C)
>
> "There's nothing to do in the evenings, is there?" (F25D)
>
> "I don't do anything. I just have my supper as quick as I can and have a wash, and then it's time to go to bed." (F20D)
>
> "You can't go out, can you? There's not time, by the time you've got home and washed and changed. You can't go straight out in the clothes you've been working in." (F30D)
>
> "I go straight to bed. I'm almost dead, by the time I get home evenings." (F20I)
>
> "Well, I just have a tidy up. I might go out a little walk if it's nice, but it's bedtime, time you've looked round." (F40D)

There are a certain number—perhaps about ten per cent—who will go out most evenings, at any cost. The destination is almost always a dance of some kind—and, as we have said, practically every evening there is a dance of some sort or another. Going to the pictures is impossible except at weekends, as the last house starts an hour before it would be possible to get there on weekdays. In the main, social activities of all kinds have to be left for the weekend.

WEEKENDS

One Monday at the beginning of March, after a fairly fine weekend, eight girls and women living at home were asked how they had spent the previous Saturday and Sunday. The weekend had nothing special about it, and had been chosen quite at random, as had also the subjects questioned. The answers, therefore, probably give a fairly typical picture of the way in which weekends are spent by girls living at home.

Helen (F25C, lives alone with her mother in a small house in a town ten miles away. Worked in a factory there before she came here):

> "I was too tired on Saturday to do anything. On Sunday I got up about ten and did some of my mending. We don't

have much breakfast on Sundays, we both like to have a lie in. Mother cooked some dinner—I meant to help her, but I was mending, and I sort of got settled, you know, in the chair, I didn't feel like getting out of it. Mother didn't mind, she's very good to me.

"In the afternoon I went to the pictures, but I'd seen the film before, so I was sorry I'd bothered. It wasn't worth it, with all the queuing. Then I came back and had my tea, and I went to bed early. It's the only chance you get of an early night, Sundays. I sometimes go to a dance on Saturday nights, but it's always so crowded you can't get in."

BETTY (F20D, one of a large family living in the same town. Most of her brothers and sisters are younger than herself, and she has always to help with them a good deal. Tobacconist's assistant before she came here):

"I didn't come in Saturday. I went to a dance on Friday night, with Mary, and it was very late, so I stopped with her Friday night, and so we neither of us woke up Saturday morning. We missed the bus. Oh, we had a lovely day Saturday. We just mucked about all the morning, and then in the afternoon we went shopping. I got some lovely wool for my jumper—a lovely shade of red, like dark rose, if you know what I mean, only a real red, not pink. Only one coupon for the eight ounces. Then we went to the pictures, and there were two fellows there Mary used to know at work. They're in the R.A.M.C. now, quite nice fellows they were, and we all had fish and chips. I didn't think there'd be any fish left, it was nearly eleven o'clock, they've usually sold out long before then. Funny, wasn't it, on a Saturday night, they still had all that fish.

"I got up at a quarter to ten on Sunday and helped my mother, for a change! She gets fed up, no one to help her all the week. It was a lovely day, I did want to go out, go for a walk to the aerodrome, it's lovely round that way, but I didn't like to go by myself. I just went out a little walk in the afternoon, just to get a bit of fresh air, and that's all I did."

MARJORIE (F30C. Married. She and husband live in half of small house in the town. She has a little boy of six, staying with her sister in Leicester):

"Do you know, we're terrible. We never go out, my husband and I. He didn't get home till eight o'clock on Saturday, so I had a good tidy up when I got in, and had a look through my summer clothes. I wanted to see what I'd got I could cut up for a suit for my little boy. He's a terrible one, he grows out of all his clothes. My sister says he's hardly got a thing he can wear, he's growing so. I thought I might be able to make him a little suit from one of my old dresses. I've got a blue linen one that I can't wear any more, that would do ever so well, but I don't know when I'll get the time to make it, I'm sure. You can't bring that sort of work in to do dinner times, can you? It's not like knitting.

"On Sunday I had a real good lie in. I never got up till dinner time. My husband brought me my cup of tea, and he said: 'Don't you get up till dinner time, you're tired out.' I felt that lazy—you know, I just lay there, and never even had a look at the paper. My husband was at work this Sunday, so I didn't have no dinner to cook. I got up in the afternoon and did a bit of mending, and wrote a letter to my sister. I never went out, except just to post the letter, and when my husband came in he said, 'You've done a lot, haven't you!'—you know, laughing. 'Yes,' I said, 'Sunday's my busy day, you know!' We have a lot of little jokes, my husband and I."

LIL (F25D. Married, husband in the army. No children. Lives with her family in nearby town):

"I was going to go to the pictures on Saturday night, and then when I got in I thought no, I'd have a bath instead. So I had my bath, it was lovely and hot, and I think it must have given me a bit of a chill getting out of it, because I felt ever so bad all Sunday. I had a cold in my stomach, and I couldn't go out at all. It was a shame, it was such a nice sunny day, and I'd said to my mother only the night before: 'If it's a nice day like this tomorrow, then I'll go for a walk tomorrow afternoon. I'll go miles and miles if it's like this.'"

NANCY (F17C-D. Lives at home in the town. Third youngest of large family):

"I came out on Saturday, and my young man was waiting for me by the entrance, and we went straight off to the pictures, I didn't even have any tea. Then we came out of the pictures and went to the dance at the Catholics. I didn't get to bed till gone two.

"I was supposed to get up Sunday morning and get the breakfast, we always take turns for that, me and my sisters, and it was my turn this week. But I didn't wake up, and I heard Winnie (her younger sister) shouting for me: 'Where are you, Nance? We want our cup of tea.' I was that sleepy, I didn't take no notice of her. She come and shook me, but I still didn't take no notice. I don't think I could have done, I was like that—you know, I knew what she was doing, but I couldn't have moved or opened my eyes—you know. Next thing I knew, she'd brought me a cup of tea. She's a good kid, because it wasn't her turn.

"In the afternon my young man called for me and we went to the tea-dance at the Social Club, and then we went on to the pictures. We always make all we can of our weekends, like that. We keep on all the time, if we aren't at a dance then we're at the pictures. Well, you have to, don't you. You can't go nowhere during the week."

Margie (F20C-D. Lives at home near the town. Several brothers, all older than herself and away from home. She is the only one at home, but there are several evacuees in the house):

"It's funny, all through the week I'm saying to myself, I'll do this on Sunday, I'll do that on Sunday. Like if there's a dance on Thursday and I can't go, I say to myself: 'I'll go to the dance on Sunday.' But it's funny, when Sunday comes along I never seem to do a thing. It's gone ten before I get up, and I don't get dressed then. My mother's always on at me: 'You can't go about like that in your dressing-gown, suppose somebody was to come in?' But I don't know, I can't seem to manage any other way. I do my bit of washing, and yesterday I had a dress and a pair of stockings to mend before I could put them on. Then in the afternoon I write to my brother. I should have written to two of them, really, but the time seemed to run away so, I don't know how it is, Sundays. I meant to go to the pictures in the evening, but I thought to myself, 'Well, I don't know.' And I didn't trouble."

Sadie (F20D, described earlier, p. 40). Lives with parents in a nearby town. Only child):

"Oh, I had a lovely weekend. I didn't come to work on Saturday, I went to stay with a friend all the weekend. I went on Friday night, and didn't come back till this morning. Oh, I had a lovely time. You wouldn't know there was a war on where she lives. She's on a farm, and we had cream every day, and lovely fresh eggs, and all the milk you could drink. I had a cup of cocoa every night made with all milk. I love cocoa like that, don't you, made with all milk?"

MYRA (F25D. Married, husband in army. Lives with family in a nearby town):

"I had such a disappointment this weekend. My husband was to have forty-eight hours' leave, and then Friday night I got a wire to say he couldn't come. Oh, I could have cried my eyes out. I'd been getting all worked up for it—you know. I'd bought myself a new pair of stockings, and I've sat up every evening to finish my cardigan, and I'd just finished it when the wire came. It's blue—a sort of powder blue, that's his favourite colour on me. I couldn't put it on. My mother said: 'Why don't you put it on, see how it looks, now you've finished it?' But I couldn't do it. I'd got it all planned I was going to put it on when he come home, I just hadn't any heart for it. Just pushed it away in my drawer as if it was one of my old things, I never even held it up to see how it looked.

"I don't know how I've got through the weekend. My mother says I've been looking half dopey, and I wouldn't be surprised. Oh, I've been miserable."

One comment must be made here. The weekend to which these accounts refer is one *before* the change in weekend hours. Thus, at this time the girls were stopping work at eight-thirty on both Friday and Saturday, whereas later the hours were changed, and we stopped at eight on Friday, the same as every other week day, and at midday on Saturday. Thus the ritual of Saturday afternoon shopping does not appear in the above accounts, for at that time shopping was done by local girls in a hurried manner on either Friday or Saturday, while girls living in other towns and villages were unable to do any at all on either day, as the shops were closed before they got back. Since then, Saturday afternoon shopping has become something of an institution, and forms a major topic of conversation during the latter days of the week. The chances are that one will meet every single person one knows in the High Street at some time or another on that afternoon.

We will now go on to give some details of the way in which the girls' money is spent, on these afternoons and otherwise.

THE WEEKLY BUDGET

An ordinary unskilled girl gets about £2 14*s*. in her pay packet each week, including overtime. Naturally enough, the girls we are discussing in this chapter—i.e. those living at home—are better off financially than those in lodgings (cf. p. 104). They do, of course, pay something into the general family fund, but—with a few exceptions—they pay no more now than they did before, when they had much lower-paid jobs. Thus a girl who was formerly getting 23/- a week for some sort of domestic work, and paid her mother 10/- of this, will in all probability, still pay her mother 10/- out of her new wage of £2 14*s*. Most parents who are at all in a position to do so, accept, and indeed encourage this state of affairs, feeling that after working such long hours, the girl deserves to keep the money herself. On the average, then, the basic weekly expense of a girl living at home will be:

To mother, 10/- to 15/-
To canteen (if not provided with sandwiches from homes), 10/-
Fares, 3/-.

She will thus be left with more than a pound to spend as she likes. About three or four shillings of this will probably be spent on pictures or dances; about five shillings saved—usually for some special coveted article, like a summer coat, or a new pair of shoes. The rest is spent on the Saturday afternoon shopping expeditions referred to above.

As this seems to account for a big share of the weekly money—anything up to fifteen shillings or one pound—it seemed worth while to get some idea of exactly how the money was being spent on these expeditions. So some typical individual shopping lists were recorded—partly from observation, and partly from conversation:

(1) F25C (unmarried):

Tube Glymiel jelly	1/9
Cigarettes	6½
Tube of wine gums	2
Small tin Milk of Magnesia tablets	7

Large bottle of cough mixture	1/9
1 pair of stockings	4/11
	9/8½

(The stockings turn out to be already laddered, so she has to go out during the dinner hour on Monday to change them.)

(2) F25D (married):

Nail varnish	1/4
Card of hooks and eyes	4
Jar of cold cream	2/6
Shampoo	6
Tablet of soap	4
4 stamps	10
Pair of No. 9 knitting needles	8
Cigarettes	1/6
	8/-

(3) F25C (unmarried):

Shampoo and set at hairdresser	4/6
Pair of dance shoes	12/11
Polish remover	1/9
Ornamental flower for dance dress	2/6
Writing pad	7½
	£1 2 3½

(4) F20D (unmarried):

Knitting pattern	3
No. 8 needles	8
Hand cream	2/6
Pair of stockings	3/1
Iron tonic	1/7
	8/1

(5) F20C (unmarried):

8 oz. Wool for jumper	7/5
Pair No. 10 needles	6
Pair of stockings	3/6
Shoes from mender	5/11
Jar cold cream	2/6

Jar vanishing cream	1/6
Box of powder	1/6
Tube of toothpaste	7½
Tube of camphor ice	10½
Cigarettes	2/5
Mending wool	8
Ribbon	1/5
Toffee	5
Shoe laces	7
	£1 9 10

(6) F25D (unmarried):

Woman's World	3
Ankle socks	2/1
Knickers	4/11
Cold cream	1/3
Soap	3
	8/9

(7) F30C (married):

Knitting wool for little boy's jersey	5/11
Safety pins	2
Packet of needles	2
Bias binding	7
Shampoo	3
Lipstick	1/1
Halibut oil	2/-
Packet of rusks (tried to get biscuits)	1/4
Cigarettes	2/1
	13/7

(8) F20C (unmarried):

Writing pad and envelopes	1/11
Knitting pattern	3
Box of powder	2/-
Jar of night cream	1/7
Stamps	1/8
Reel of cotton	2
Bottle of ink	6
Swiss roll (to send to boy friend in Army)	9
Cigarettes	2/9
	11/7

(9) F25D (married):

Box of throat lozenges	6
Embroidered tablecloth	18/5
	18/11

Says: "It's my sister's birthday to-morrow, and I wanted to get her something she wanted, and she told me she wanted a pretty tea cloth. I didn't know it could cost all that; I don't know what I'll do for next week, I'll have nothing left."

Even from this small number of lists, it is possible to see clearly the emphasis on cosmetics, knitting, cigarettes, etc. There would also be a heavy emphasis on sweets, if there were any to be had; one of the staple topics of conversation on Saturday mornings is whether or not there will be any sweets left in the shops by the afternoon. There rarely are.

Cosmetics also are much discussed. There is always great excitement when the news goes round that some particularly popular brand of any kind of cosmetic is in stock somewhere:

"They've got some Coty powder in J's."

"What do you mean, real Coty? In the Coty boxes?"

"I think so. I haven't been but Lil went dinner time, and she got a lovely box."

"What shades have they got?"

"I don't know . . ."

"Are there any dark shades? I want a dark powder for the summer."

"I shan't worry about the colour. So long as it's Coty, that's all I care. I'll mix it to make the right colour."

"Will it still be there to-morrow? Was there a lot?"

"I don't know. Lil said . . ."

"I'm not going to chance it. I'm going to get off early to-night."

"It's worth it for Coty, isn't it? You don't see that much now."

There are practically no housekeeping goods bought at all on these expeditions. The reason, of course, is that, from the nature of their work, none of these women, married or single, are able to look after their homes themselves, and so whoever it is who looks after the house for them also does the household shopping during the week. In fact, those shopping lists provide by themselves a perfect illustration of the point made earlier—that this type of factory work fosters an attitude of carefree irresponsibility to every aspect of daily life.

There are, of course, a small number of women who are so situated that they undertake serious household shopping on Saturday afternoons; but they are so few as not to appear in a random sample of this size. For them, the scheme being considered by the management, of providing a store in the factory for the purchase of essentials like bread, groceries, etc., would prove a great boon.[1] But it is clear from the above that for the majority, any such scheme would be superfluous. Their shopping is focused on personal and luxury goods, outside the scope of such a scheme.

II

IN BILLETS

THE BILLETING CAPACITY of the town is strained to the limit. On top of its quota of evacuees from blitzed cities, the town has had to house both factory and Air Ministry workers who have been coming in in hundreds. As always where there are more lodgers than there are willing landladies, relations between the two tend to be strained, but here this natural tension is aggravated by several subsidiary factors.

In the first place, however, it is necessary to distinguish between the different *c asses* of billeted worker. It seemed to be a fairly consistent rule that the D-class workers got on with their landladies much better than did the C- and B-. This is natural enough, as most of the houses hereabouts are of D-type from the point of view of the town dweller (i.e. the kitchen is the main sitting-room, there is no bathroom, and only candles upstairs); and while this was nothing new to D-class billetees, it was a constant source of grievance, directly and indirectly, to the C-B types. Another less obvious reason for the difference in attitude is related to that discussed in the first chapter of this section. The C-B-classes were much more conscious of the temporary nature of their stay there, and also

[1] Not yet in operation. Here local apathy is largely to blame. Of twenty-eight food retailers recently invited to a meeting to discuss workers' shopping problems, only seven turned up and they failed to suggest anything constructive, in spite of appeals by the Ministry of Labour—(*Works Manager*).

had more chance of going to their own homes at weekends. Thus they were not compelled, as were the D-classes, to settle down and make the best of it; on the contrary, they lived in a constant atmosphere of makeshift and impending change—an atmosphere favourable to the growth and flourishing of grievances. For with the possibility of change for ever round the corner, one can afford to dislike places and people almost without limit; whereas if one feels that the situation is permanent, one feels more inclined to try and learn to like at least something about it.

Some very good examples of this unsettled, discontented attitude occurred in an observer's billet, which for this reason is perhaps worth describing, although the house itself is not very typical.

It is a tall, rather forbidding-looking red brick house near the centre of the town. It is run by a middle-aged C-class couple whose pre-war profession was farming, but who are now thinking of letting rooms and catering as a permanent profession. Unlike most of the houses, it has a bathroom, in which the water is heated by a very ancient type of gas copper, which heats very slowly—it takes between one and two hours to heat enough water for a bath. Unlike most of the billets, too, it has a separate sitting-room for the lodgers, who have all their meals there, instead of in the kitchen with the landlady's family. This room is in the basement, rather small and rather crowded with furniture, including a number of straight-backed chairs, which are placed in a row against one wall, giving a rather dismal waiting-room effect.

At the time when she was there, the three other permanent lodgers were all of the B-C type just referred to. First there is Mr. T., a weather-beaten regular officer, now working in the War Ministry. He is a constant talker, his conversation consisting almost entirely of grumbles about the billet, and an unlimited supply of "stories" which he has collected from all over the world. Then there is Miss V., a demure sort of woman in her early thirties. She works in the factory in one of the higher departments, takes the work very seriously, and is always studying technical books about it. Mr. F. is a lively, self-assured little man of about thirty. He also works at some skilled technical job in the factory, but only temporarily. He loathes being there, loathes the town and the billet and the people, and thinks about nothing but getting back to his home town for weekends.

The following scene, one Friday evening, illustrates exactly the B-C attitude to life here.

It is a bitterly cold evening, towards the end of February. The fire is very low, and at the moment is rather smothered by small coal and slack. Miss V. is sitting over it, reading. Mr. T. comes in, dressed in Home Guard uniform, and rubbing his hands together:

"Cor stiffen the crows!" he exclaims. "Look at the fire! I'm going to find myself another billet. I shall die of cold if I stay here much longer."

"We could ask for some more coal," suggested Miss V.

"Ask for some more coal! Do you call that coal? It's a shovelful of dirt out of the garden, if you ask me. And they damped it down at that! It's no use asking for anything here. If you say anything, they'll tell you there's a war on, and it's patriotic to be cold. *They're* doing all right in there (indicating the kitchen) with their lovely warm stove. I've seen them! And then they tell us there's a coal shortage! That would be all very fine if the landlady was cold too, but there's a catch in it somewhere. I've met that sort of thing before."

"In my last digs we used to bring in a sack of coal for ourselves," says Miss V.

"What, when we're paying thirty bob a week? I'd rather freeze to death than supply them with coal! No, I'm not going to stay here much longer. I shall move off to —— and stay with my cousin. It'll be difficult travelling, but it would be better than staying here to be frozen and starved to death. Where's little Jump-to-it gone?"

"He said he was going up to the Three Cows."

"I don't blame him. There's nothing worth drinking, but they do have a decent fire up there. I'd go myself, but I'm not going to turn out into that wind again."

Mr. T. draws up a chair the other side of the fire and cowers over it rubbing his hands, and continues:

"Look at that supper she gave us, too. The meat was so tough I couldn't even cut it. I think it's the same as we had yesterday, I couldn't eat any of that at all. I suppose she'll come in and say: 'You're not a big meat eater, are you?' I shall say if she does, I shall say: 'I like meat all right, but I can't eat shoe leather.'"

"I think she keeps it hot too long," says Miss V. "I think she cooks it in the middle of the day, and then heats it up for each of us as we come in. I must say I don't think it's good enough. I think thirty shillings is too much to pay for sharing a room, and all these discomforts."

"Of course it's too much! Five bob would be too much for a hole like this. Snivelling snakes and cross-eyed crocodiles! (peculiar exclamations are a hobby of his). I'm going to put my coat on."

He gets up, and puts on his Home Guard overcoat, which is hanging over a chair. As he does so, he catches sight of a piece of bread left on someone's plate on the supper table. He snatches it up and throws it in the fire:

"They even feed their bloody chickens off us," he says, as he does so. "Well, that's one bit less for Mrs. Scrounge when she comes in to see what we've left."

He walks back to his chair, humming:

"And every day a holiday
Because you're married to me—Cor blimey!"

He sits down heavily in the chair, and muses on:

"I wish I knew what was happening to our points. I haven't seen anything of the points yet in this place."

"Those prunes we had are off the points."

"Prunes? I wouldn't eat muck like that if I ever had a decent meal here, but you have to have something to fill you up. I suppose she'd tell us that the beans for breakfast are off the points too. About seven beans on a plate, that's what we get. We ought to have the butter and margarine on the table. Everyone else does. She can't say she wants that for cooking; what are the cooking fats for?

"If I had to stay here much longer she'd hear something about it. I could promise her that."

"If I was going to stay here, one thing I'd insist on . . ."

At this moment Mr. F. comes in, back from the Three Cows, shivering with cold.

"As he comes ro-olling home," sings Mr. T. loudly. "Have a good time up there?"

Mr. F. shrugs his shoulders.

"Thank the Lord I'll be out of this place to-morrow. This time to-morrow—let me see, what will I be doing? I know, I will be having a hot bath, not a tepid drizzle from that dirty old wreck upstairs. Then I'll have a nice fire in my room, and on Sunday morning I'll have my breakfast in bed—nice crisp bacon, and toast, and coffee. I'll think of you people shivering here, falling up and down the stairs with candles——"

"Never mind, the weekend after that I'll be gone too," says Miss V. "I think I'm going to go most weekends. It's not a very long journey, is it."

She and Mr. F. fall to discussing ways and means of getting to and from London. Mr. T. continues to cower over the fire, hunched up in his Home Guard overcoat:

"Snivelling snakes and cross-eyed crocodiles! This is good practice for a concentration camp anyway," he mutters.

Now, the point about this conversation (and it was not exceptional; a lot of evenings were spent almost entirely on talk like this) is the attitude it indicates of ineffective grumbling and dislike. Not one of the speakers had any intention of trying to alleviate their real and imagined hardships; we never once heard any of them mention any of these points to the landlady. The one idea was simply to get away, as soon as and as often as possible.

Among the D-classes this sort of attitude is definitely less common—partly because of lack of money for weekend travelling, and partly because they have not been brought up to the idea that such frequent travelling is possible. And, of course, most of them are living in with the landlady as one of the family, using the kitchen as their sitting-room, so that any grumbles are likely to be made *to* her rather than *about* her, so that there is some chance of some kind of solution being hammered out between them.

And there are grumbles, of course. The main ones are as follows:

(i) FOOD

There is always a certain amount of feeling that landladies are not providing their lodgers with a full share of rations. Whether this is actually the case or not is usually quite impossible to say, for the landlady naturally lumps all the rations together, for her own family and for the lodgers, and cooks with them for the whole lot. As there is no way of proving anything one way or the other, the bone of contention remains, and one continually hears this sort of remark:

"I never see my butter. The bread is spread before it comes to table, and I know it's always margarine."

"I didn't get my egg this fortnight. I don't know what's happened to it."

"We only get meat on Sundays. You'd have thought there'd be enough for a bit of stew or something during the week, wouldn't you?"

Some of the girls, too, object to their landladies' universal preference for providing a midday dinner and then just a light supper in the evening. This means that if the girl is to get the full value of her board she has to dash home during the dinner hour, gobble the meal in ten minutes or so, and dash back again:

"I did have to rush my dinner today, it was a shame. I had to leave my pudding, it was syrup pudding; I'm ever so fond of syrup pudding. It's an awful rush getting back every day, but my landlady wouldn't take anything off for it. If I don't have my dinner midday with her, well, I'm just unlucky, that's all." (F20D)

Some landladies provide sandwiches for midday instead, but this, of course, provides almost infinite scope for complaint about the quantity and quality of the contents. A very common complaint about them is that stale bread is used:

"It's always dry by the time I get them. One day the bread was so stale I couldn't eat them. I told her, and she just told me there was a war on. Then Mrs. C., who is staying there with me, she said the bread was stale. She saw the loaf my landlady was cutting, and she told her it was too stale; she told my landlady that, but she just said, 'Well, I can't help it. She'll have to put up with it.'" (F25D)

(ii) LACK OF PRIVACY

Most billets consist of a candle-lit bedroom and a share of the common kitchen-sitting-room. This is a source of complaint for C rather than D girls, who resent having their landlady's eye on everything they do:

"I was sitting there mending my stockings, and she didn't say anything, but I could see she was saying to herself: 'I wonder where she got those stockings from? I wonder how much she paid for them?' I could just see her puzzling it out to herself." (F30C)

"Sometimes my mother sends me a parcel from home, and as soon as I get in, it's: 'Oh, Peggy, you've got a parcel!' and she stands over me while I undo it, and sees everything I take out. Sometimes my mother sends me a cake, or a piece of chocolate; well, I'm not greedy, and I wouldn't mind giving her a bit, but when she stands over me like that, counting what you've got—well, it's not very nice. If I offer her a bit later on I know she's thinking to herself: 'Well, that's not a very big bit, out of all you've got!'" (F20C)

"I don't know, I get fed up sometimes. Sometimes you come home in the evenings and you don't feel like talking—you know, you're a bit tired. When I'm feeling like that, just come in and sit down sort of thing, they're all whispering to each other, 'Isn't she in a temper?' 'What's the matter with her?' Just because I don't happen to feel like talking to them." (F25C)

This is particularly felt by girls from large towns, who are accustomed to an impersonal attitude from neighbours.

(iii) DIFFICULTY OF HAVING FRIENDS IN BILLETS

A very common form of invitation heard is: "Come round Sunday afternoon. My landlady will be out till six, I've got the place to myself." For it is difficult to entertain friends comfortably while someone else is sitting there either bored or critical, and certainly wanting to be left in peace for Sunday afternoon. And there is always the humiliating feeling that it is impossible to ask anyone to stay even for a cup of tea, without rousing a hornet's nest of financial and rationing complications with the landlady.

(iv) COMING IN AT NIGHT

There is inevitably a certain amount of friction between girls who want to come in late and landladies who want to go to bed early. Most of them are rather reluctant to part with keys—especially if they have a number of people in the house all wanting keys. A few of them disapprove of girls being out after ten or so on principle; but with most of them it is just a question of inconvenience; either some more keys have to be made and continually checked up on, or else someone has to stay up and let the girls in. Although all these complications are pretty widespread, there is among the more D-class girls nothing like the practically non-stop grumbling quoted earlier in this chapter. Indeed many of them, while they grumble intermittently about these sort of things, are most of the time on good terms with their landladies, and speak of them like this:

"She's a dear old thing really. She's funny, some ways, but I like her. I wouldn't want to move." (F25D)

"Sometimes I get fed up, but she's good to me really, and I like the kiddies." (F30D)

"She's like a mother to me. If I stop in bed on a Sunday morning, she'll bring me a cup of tea." (F20D)

(v) EVENINGS AND WEEKENDS

These are spent by billeted girls in much the same way as by girls living at home (as described in the last chapter). There are, however, certain differences. There is much more *aimless* going out by girls living in billets—going out simply for the sake of not being cooped up all the evening in a kitchen with a landlady whom she may or may not like:

"I don't know what I'm going to do this evening. I did want to get on with making my blouse, but she (landlady) gets on my nerves so, sitting staring at me. She'll sit for an hour sometimes, just watching me. She doesn't read a paper, she doesn't knit, she doesn't do anything. Just sits and watches me while I eat my dinner and then watches what I do next, if I'm knitting or sewing or what it is. It's enough to drive you potty. That's why if I don't go out I go to bed early. I sometimes try to write letters after I've gone to bed, but I've only got a candle up there. She's a terror with letters. If I'm sitting in my chair writing a letter she'll walk past twenty times, has a good look each time what I'm writing. Any other evening she'll sit there and never stir, but if I'm writing a letter she's up and down all the time, you'd wonder what's the matter with her." (F20D)

"She always had a good look at all my letters that come. This morning she called up to me: 'You've got two letters,

Molly, one from Jack and one from your sister.' 'How do you know it's from my sister?' I asked her. 'It says so on the back,' she says. See? She'd looked at the back, and she'd looked at the postmark—she'd done everything bar open it!

"I don't know, I'm fed up. I don't feel like going out tonight, but I don't want to stop in with her. I suppose I'll go out somewhere." (F20C)

"I'm fed up with going out every evening, but we can't stay in, my landlady wants the kitchen most days. I'm so tired, I don't feel like going to a dance tonight. Do you know what I'd like? I'd like just to go back and curl myself up in front of the fire with my knitting, and him in the armchair with his pipe, and have a nice quiet evening. But what I've really got to do, I've got to rush back and wash myself in the scullery, and put on my dance dress. It's going to be another late night again." (F20C)

At weekends there is less lounging about than among girls living at home. At home one can rely on having a fairly pleasant time by simply letting oneself drift. Among familiar surroundings there is always something to do, and among one's own friends and family there is always someone to talk to. But a girl in billets is driven to *plan* her weekends more. She knows that unless she arranges for something to happen, nothing will happen.

(vi) THE WEEKLY BUDGET

The average billet costs about twenty-five shillings a week, including breakfast, dinner and some kind of supper. Her basic expenses are thus greater than those of a girl living at home; she is also worse off in a number of incidental ways. For one thing, she has to buy for herself all the little oddments which are usually to be found lying around in most homes; needles, ink; a tube of glue, string. Also, for the reasons indicated above, she is likely to spend more on dances, cinemas, etc., for lack of anywhere else congenial to be. And above all, for all those for whom it is even remotely possible, there is the eternal preoccupation of saving enough money to go home for a weekend at the earliest possible date.[1]

[1] *Food, meals and leisure.* This very realistic description of billeting conditions is not entirely news to Management; the position has been growing steadily worse since the better billets became absorbed. The Social Centre was, of course, an attempt to provide an alternative to hanging around the billet

12

AT THE HOSTEL

THE HOSTEL IS situated about three miles out of the town, at the top of a winding country lane, and workers are collected and taken home by bus. Formerly it was an ordinary private house, but now one wing is occupied by the manager and his wife, and the other has been converted into a hostel for girls working in the factory. At present there are only ten of them there, but considerable expansion is expected soon.

At first sight conditions are ideal. The girls have an attractive, well-built country house to live in, and the run of extensive grounds outside. They have a large, comfortably furnished sitting-room to themselves, with a blazing fire to welcome them in the evenings. Adjoining this room is the dining-room, with french windows opening on to a lawn and an attractive garden. There is almost always a vase of flowers on each of the two tables. Upstairs are comfortable roomy bedrooms, with two or three beds in each, and much more drawer and cupboard space than is ever found in a billet. In the bathroom and washing room there is an unlimited supply of hot water at all hours. The girls are looked after by a housekeeper and two maids, who between them produce excellent meals morning and evening. For all this they pay only twenty-two shillings and sixpence a week. Any journalist looking over the place for a few hours would have every excuse for going home and writing up a sunshine story about wartime hostel life in the most glowing terms he could conjure up for the occasion.

---

after working hours, and at the present time tea, biscuits, and light refreshments are available; the idea being to encourage billetees to get out of their billets as much as possible.

Meals, however, are entirely separate and a much more difficult problem. Some six months ago, at the instigation of the Ministry of Labour, and with the support of the Production Ministry and Ministries of Health and Food, an approach was made to the local Council with a view to getting them to open a British Restaurant. This would have enabled compulsory billeting to be introduced, but what is more important, would have eased the food problems of those persons taking in billetees. Moreover, the facility for obtaining meals at weekends in the case of married couples, where both work at the factory, would be advantageous.

Apparently the sole authority capable of initiating such a British Restaurant is the Municipal Council, and as long as they steadfastly refuse to make a move, this most valuable adjunct to welfare facilities in a country town will be lacking—(*Works Manager*).

And yet when one lives there, a different picture comes to light. A picture of endless grumbling and bickering; a picture of backbiting and tale-bearing; of feuds between girls and staff, and between one set of girls and another. The real excellence of material conditions is almost lost to sight amid the welter of ill-temper and discontent which characterises life here.

To understand the reasons for this, a short description of the girls and their attitude to their lives is necessary. At the time when we were there, most of the ten girls were C-class, in their early twenties. Two were definitely B-class, and one on the border between B and C. None of them had been here long (the hostel was only started a few weeks before) and none of them had had any previous experience of factory life or work.

The first thing to strike a newcomer about these girls, as a group, is the lack of initiative they display about their leisure. It is true that the hostel is three miles out of the town, and one can understand unwillingness to walk home late at night along three miles of dark country lanes. But there was plenty of opportunity for leisure activities inside the hostel. The rules allowed any girl to have any visitors she liked on any evening. She could invite them to supper for a small extra charge on her weekly bill, and on Saturdays and Sundays she could have them there for any or all of the time. As far as the rules were concerned, there was unlimited scope for parties and social evenings of all kinds. Yet never once, in all the weeks' observation, did any of the girls invite any guests, male or female, up to the hostel. And practically never did any of them go out themselves on a weekday evening. The following is a typical account of the way in which weekday evenings were spent here.

It is nine o'clock on a Thursday evening. Supper is just over, and someone has turned on the wireless in the sitting-room, and four of the girls are sitting round the fire, in armchairs or on the sofa. During supper there has been a lot of talk about who is to have a bath tonight and who isn't, and three of the girls have already gone off to have their baths and go to bed. Two others are still sitting in the dining-room over the remains of the meal and talking about some friends they both know at home. Another is doing some ironing downstairs.

In the sitting-room at the moment there is no talking. Barbara, a fair-haired B-class girl, fresh from school and very earnest, is sitting writing a letter home. Betty, a twenty-year-old C-class girl, plump and cheerful, is knitting a green jumper for herself with an expression of great concentration. The other two, both C-class and twenty-five years old, are sitting doing nothing at all, one in an armchair and the other on the sofa. One of them hums vaguely to the wireless.

The nine o'clock news starts.

"Is that nine o'clock?" says Gwen, one of the two girls just mentioned. "I ought to get my stockings to mend. Do you know, I won't have a pair to put on tomorrow. Those new ones I got, there's a great ladder all up one of them."

"What a shame. How did you do it?"

"I don't know, that's the puzzle. I suddenly felt it start to run—you know how you can just feel it sometimes, and I looked and there it was. All up the front. I couldn't wear them."

"You must have caught it on something."

"But I didn't. I know I didn't. I'm always careful like that. I'm not like some, don't look where I'm going."

"What a shame. I ought to do mine too, but I'm not going to. I'm going to take them home, they'll do them for me over the weekend."

Pause. Gwen picks up the paper and looks at it for a minute. Yawns.

"I'm proper tired tonight. Think I'll go up soon."

"So am I. I'm fed up. I thought I'd get a phone call this evening. I thought they'd have rung me up from home."

"Why, did they say they were going to this evening?"

"No, but they must have got my letter by now, telling them I wasn't well, and I'd have thought they'd have rung up to see how I was."

"Perhaps they will do. It's not half-past yet."

"No, they won't ring now. If they don't ring by quarter-past nine I know they aren't going to. They have to go across to the phone, see, and she don't like being disturbed after nine. Not a lot after."

At about a quarter to ten Barbara puts away her writing things, says "good night" in her gentle voice, and goes up to bed. Roused by this from her lethargy, Gwen also gets up and fetches a kettle to boil for her hot-water bottle.

"Is that for your bottle?" says Betty, looking up. "Isn't the water hot?"

"It's hot enough for a bath, Cissie says, but it's not hot enough for a bottle. Not a good hot bottle. I like them real hot."

"Oh. I'll get mine then."

The two girls from the dining-room come in now, and hearing the news about the water, go and get their bottles. The four of them sit round the fire watching for the kettle to boil. When it does, two of the bottles are filled, and Gwen goes to refill the kettle for the other two.

"They might have the water hot for the bottles," she says. "A cold night like this, you'd have thought they'd keep it boiling for us."

"It's that creature in the kitchen. She grudges every bit of coal she puts on the fire. That time when I couldn't get no hot water for my bath, I went and told her about it, and she flew out at me: 'They've had four baths already this evening,' she says. 'Well, I can't help that,' I told her. 'I haven't had my bath, and I didn't have one last night. There's nine of us here,' I told her, 'you ought to cater for nine of us, not four.'"

"What did she say?"

"Went off and saw Mrs. G. (the manager's wife) of course. I suppose I'll get told off again. They always pick on me. Why don't they tell *her* off when things go wrong? It's her fault. She's supposed to run things here."

The kettle boils, and the remaining two bottles are filled; by a quarter past ten everyone has gone to bed.

The sort of grumbling quoted at the end of this description is a characteristic feature of every evening's conversation. Usually it is about the food, and includes complaints which to an outsider looking at the meals supplied, would seem quite absurd. A hot meat or fish meal is provided every night, and for breakfast there is always something like bacon or fish or egg, a cereal, and unlimited quantities of butter or margarine put on the table for people to help themselves to as much as they like. Nevertheless, one is continually hearing remarks like this:

"I don't know what happens to all the money we pay here. My mother says that the whole of the rations you can get on one book only costs two shillings and threepence a week—

that's all you can get for one person. So they're making a pound a week on each of us!"

"It's that woman in the kitchen. She can't do her job. The rotten meals she gives us, it ought to be reported to somewhere high up, the way we're treated here."

"They think that anything will do for us; we're only the workers."

"Why can't we have a tin of fruit or something decent for a sweet? She's got all our points—why can't we have a fruit salad with them?"

There are definitely no material grounds for these complaints. As in the canteen, the food provided at the hostel is better than anything that could be obtained outside. And, as in the case of the canteen, one of the reasons for the complaining is conscious or unconscious snobbery; the mixture of classes ranging from B to lower C intensifies this. Another reason is the personal friction between the girls and the housekeeper at the hostel. She is at heart a good-natured woman, and competent at her job, but she is also quick-tempered and easily takes offence. Thus she can't bring herself to laugh at and ignore these absurd complaints whenever they occur (and they are usually spoken in an idle and unthinking manner), but magnifies them into serious and thought-out charges against her. This attitude reacts again on the girls, who are equally unable to laugh off her moods of exaggerated anger and offence. Thus the whole situation grows in import as it rebounds from one party to another, until a most trivial incident is magnified into a cloud that poisons the whole atmosphere, and everyone concerned is running up and down to the Management reporting on each other, telling tales, running one another down, painting contradictory and highly-coloured pictures of the mountain which some insignificant incident has by now become, until the dazed and bewildered Management is forced to make some kind of hasty decision which probably annoys everybody.

For by the time the situation has reached this stage, there is really nothing that can be done; either to ignore or to try to sort out the mainly imaginary tangle is equally disastrous. The only hope of improving matters is to get at the real cause of all these rumpuses; and that is not at all an easy matter.

For at the root of the trouble is the fact that these girls are leading irresponsible lives quite unsuited to adult human beings. All day in the factory they are doing (most of them at least) easy and quite irresponsible work. When they get home in the evening, everything has been done for them. As we have shown, this is pretty much the case with all the girls, but it is even more marked at the hostel, where it has been ordained by *authority* that they need not do a hand's turn to help themselves. They are free not only from the problems of shopping and rationing, but even from hearing discussions about them, as girls living at home are bound to do sometimes. This, combined with the comparative luxury in which they live, creates in the girls the feeling that they have a right to expect that everything they want will be provided; that there is a mysterious "they", untrammelled by wartime conditions, that has in its power to bestow, like a fairy godmother, anything that may be required. Their attitude is, in fact, almost the same as that of a child, who feels himself shielded from the outside world by grown-ups of infinite power but varying goodwill.

This feeling is well illustrated by the bewilderment and anger the girls displayed one day when the electricity all over the district was out of order—the immediate effect to them being that there was no way for the housekeeper to cook their breakfast. It seemed beyond their power to realise that this was a thing which the Management *couldn't* do anything about, any more than they could themselves. Like children, they simply felt that the all-powerful grown-ups ought to do something about it; and when they didn't, the only thing to do was grumble bitterly.

The power had gone off in the small hours of the morning, but the first we knew of it was at seven a.m. when the housekeeper brought candles to get up by. This passed off all right. But when it was learned that there was to be no breakfast at the hostel and we were to have it at the factory canteen when we arrived, the storm broke:

> "What! Aren't we even to have a cup of tea?"
>
> "But I can't do without a cup of tea before I go out! What shall we do?"
>
> "She could easily have got us something. She just didn't want to be bothered. They've got a range in there. She could have easily lit that to make us a breakfast."
>
> "We can't go out with nothing like this."
>
> "Aren't they going to give us anything at all, really?"

Such dismay seemed out of proportion, in view of the fact that according to present arrangements we would be having breakfast in the canteen in less than half an hour. But this was not the end of it. When we got to the factory we learned that all the electricity was off there too. None of the machinery was working, the lights were off, and everything naturally in a state of confusion. Failing to realise that anyone but themselves had any problems in these circumstances, the hostel girls redoubled their complaints about breakfast. The canteen was unable to supply anything till half-past eight, as all the stoves were out of order, and something had to be improvised.

"It's disgusting!"

"They told us we'd have it as soon as we got here at eight o'clock."

"Do they expect us to work all morning on nothing?"

"It's robbery. We pay enough, we ought to have breakfast at the proper time."

When the breakfast arrived at half-past eight—a rasher of bacon each, bread and butter and tea—complaints were renewed:

"Only one rasher!"

"You can't hardly see it!"

"No fried bread."

"It's because they aren't getting anything out of it. They'd give us a proper breakfast if we were paying them!"

Now, these girls were not, as individuals, particularly self-centred people. It was simply that hostel life of this sort gives one the feeling of living under the auspices of an all-powerful organisation whose function it is to see that nothing goes wrong, and that everything happens according to plan. The idea of having to fend for oneself is forgotten, and the reaction to any emergency is not the exercise of ingenuity and improvisation, but helpless grumbling until somebody does something about it.

Combined with this is the fact that most of them had had little experience of domestic or organisational problems. The suggestion that it is "easy" to clear out and light a long-disused old-fashioned range and cook a breakfast for ten on it in a space of twenty minutes did not strike any of them as being unreasonable.

The situation is further aggravated by the same attitude that billeted people show to life here; the attitude of living for the next weekend, of going home. This attitude necessarily involves a failure to come to grips with the problems of the away-from-home life, and one of the symptoms of this is to grumble at instead of to cope with anything unpleasant that may occur.

The solution to these difficulties is not to pander to the grumbling and try to bring material conditions even nearer to the luxury level; nor is it to cut down on the pampering and blindly Spartanise everything. What is wanted is to give the girls some kind of serious responsibility for their own lives. If this were done, whether the lives were luxurious or the reverse would matter very little.[1]

[1] It is gratifying to be able to add that conditions have undergone a considerable change for the better since the above observation. The increase in numbers from twelve to thirty partly provided the co-operative spirit, and the inhabitants have settled down very well. Even in spite of initial trouble, not a single case occurred of a Hostel girl asking to be transferred to a billet in the town.

Food grumbles are of the same order as in the Canteen; they mainly arise out of perverted sense of snobbery. Facilities for inviting boy friends to tea on Sunday and a general settling down have indicated that time solves this sort of problem as some others, but an outstanding factor has been the extent to which a nucleus of two or three girls of fairly strong character have helped to create a sufficient but unconscious spirit of leadership to make such Hostel experiments well worth while.

The girls, however, still do not fend for themselves, and it is very doubtful whether the Hostel could be successfully run if the inhabitants were allowed or encouraged to participate in domestic arrangements—(*Works Manager*).

SECTION IV

CONCLUSION

13

SOME TOPICAL PROBLEMS

THE PURPOSE OF this study has been to bring to light something of the human foundations on which any scheme for improving efficiency and increasing output here must be based. The picture of these foundations is not reassuring. We find as its material, gangs of bewildered and mainly reluctant girls, suddenly cut off from all their former interests and activities; suddenly released from almost all the social and material responsibilities which formerly gave their lives order and shape. Life has become for them a formless vista of days and weeks, from which most physical discomforts have been smoothed out, most cares lifted, and most pleasures and interests gone. Few gleams of aim or purpose lighten this vista, for their interest in the war has been blacked out by this sort of life as surely as their other interests. Instead of feeling "in it" (as the newspapers would lead one to suppose working in a war factory makes one feel) they feel out of it, in every way, more than they ever have in their lives. The "ivory tower" of the intellectuals is not more secure, more insulated from the struggles of real life, than is working twelve hours a day at an unexacting job in a humanely run war factory.

This, then, is the background of aimlessness, irresponsibility and boredom against which the organisers of this type of factory have to consider their problems. They have to consider what sort of incentives and what sort of penalties are going to be most effective in these circumstances—not what *would* be the most effective in some ideal circumstances, which in point of fact do not exist. It may be good propaganda to say that conscripted factory girls are burning with zeal to have their smack at Hitler, but it is certainly not good policy to be taken in by such propaganda and to spend time and effort on appealing to emotions which aren't there, simply because one thinks they *ought* to be there.

It is now possible to discuss in this light a few topical industrial problems.

(i) HOURS OF WORK

When the Management of a factory is suddenly called upon drastically to increase output, the simplest and most immediately effective way of doing so, is to increase the hours worked. For a short period, the individual worker will produce markedly more in a twelve-hour day than he did before in, say, a nine-hour day. But this improvement will be maintained over a length of time only in special circumstances. It is possible, under the influence of a sufficiently strong emotional drive, to work concentratedly for twelve hours a day, or more, for a very long time. But in the absence of any special emotional drive, the increase of effort called for by longer hours will very rapidly decline, until the worker is simply spreading out over a twelve-hour period almost exactly the same amount of work as he was formerly getting done in nine hours. This is a fact that has by now been established beyond question; it was proved up to the hilt during and after the last war.

This being so, the establishment of the twelve-hour day as a long-term policy only makes sense if the management has reason to suppose that there is, or can be produced in the factory, a sufficiently strong emotional incentive to ensure that these twelve hours will really be worked, and not merely dawdled away till they are equivalent to the former eight or nine hours. From the point of view of output, it does not matter at all what this incentive is. It may be patriotism; it may be money; it may be the same lively fear of penalties as kept the negro slave working in the rice fields. The only thing that matters is that the incentive should be strong, and that it should appeal to the emotions and not merely to the intellect.

Now, most managements are pretty hazy about all this; they know little about the emotions and potential emotions of their workers, and so the emotions they appeal to, and the incentives they apply, are often rather a muddle. They pay as high wages as they can afford, and hope that will encourage the workers to work harder; they appeal to patriotism, because the newspapers all do it, and it seems to be the done thing; when all else fails, they try to patch up the mess as best they can by miscellaneous and sometimes ineffective penalties.

In the case of the particular factory under discussion, it is clear enough from what has gone before that there is at present no emotional force at work capable of stimulating the girls to do twelve hours' work in a twelve-hour day. The motive of patriotism, as we have seen, is negative. The motive of wages does not apply, for there is no form of piece-work here. Penalties would have to be far more ruthless than they are anywhere in this country before they began to have any real effect; and in any case, penalties can never secure a *positive* increase in production. For penalties must always be set just below the level of the stupidest, clumsiest girl doing her best; thus a standard set by penalties alone must necessarily be considerably below what the average girl is capable of if she tries.

In the absence, then, of any effective incentive, the situation is what one might expect; between eight and nine hours' worth of work is being spread out over the twelve hours.[1]

Thus, unless some scheme can be devised for rousing enthusiasm on a scale hitherto unimagined in this factory, some degree of shortening of hours is clearly indicated. Indeed, the very fact of shortening the hours would create a situation in which there was much more chance of rousing just this required enthusiasm. For, as we have seen, a great deal of the apathy of the girls working here is due to the blackout on their own lives and interests caused by the long hours; this loss of personal interest entailing loss of social interest in general—including, of course, interest in the war. We get the unsatisfactory situation that the type of girl who takes a lively interest in her own life and social environment (i.e. the very girl who is *potentially* most capable of taking a lively interest in the war and her work) is continually at loggerheads with her job—fighting against it for the leisure which her own interests demand. Whereas the non-socially inclined, rather misfit sort of girl gets on much better, finding it rather a relief from keeping her end up in her own social environment.[2]

(ii) REST BREAKS

The normal rest breaks in this factory consist of an hour for dinner, half an hour for tea, and one ten-minute break, either in the morning or in the afternoon, according to whether dinner

[1] This may appear to be the case, but careful study has shown that the tempo of output actually increases as the day goes on, and maximum output from the Shop viewed as a whole, is definitely far higher during late afternoon and evening than in the morning. These results were obtained in Spring and Summer, and might not apply in Winter. Winter conditions are very different, and there does appear to be a strong argument for reducing hours from say October to March, if transport arrangements could be fitted in. (Summer hours average fifty-four per week)—(*Works Manager*).

[2] See accounts of Hilda and Molly in Chapter 4.

for that department is at twelve or one. This leaves, either in the morning or the afternoon, a long stretch of four or four and a half hours without an official break. Presumably the reason for this absence of a break is that the authorities fear that it would lower output. One cannot come to any dogmatic conclusion on this point without trying it out, and working out statistics about the difference. But it does seem relevant to point out that there is not a single girl, not even the most conscientious, who takes less than twenty minutes off, in one form or another, during a four-and-a-half-hour stretch of work. It surely would not be so disastrous to her final output if ten of these twenty minutes were occupied by an official break, instead of by unofficial messing about?[1]

Just general observation at the bench is enough to make one suspect that a good deal of time is being frittered away during these long spells of work; but to get more exact data, a particular girl was picked, rather more conscientious than the average, and an exact record was made of all her non-working activities during a typical Saturday morning. She is a C-class girl, about twenty-five years old, and works in the Assembly on an averagely interesting sort of job.

8 a.m. Bending down arranging her handbag, knitting, etc., in a cardboard box under the bench to keep them clean. Starts to put on her overall. Takes it off again, puts a woollen cardigan on underneath. Puts overall on. Sits down and yawns. 5 mins.

8.35 a.m. Leaning forward over the bench, her hand on her work, screwdriver poised, trying to catch conversation going on the other side of the bench about neighbour's boy friend. 1 min.

9.10 a.m. Arm on neighbour's chair back, leaning across eagerly describing her expedition to town last Saturday. Three or four others all listening intently. 3 mins.

9.30 a.m. Goes to cloakroom. Comes back, puts handbag back in cardboard box, rearranges other contents, of box. Rubs cream on her hands. 4 mins.

9.50 a.m. Stretches, tilts her chair back, holding on to the bench with straight arms. Relaxes this position

[1] This is a good suggestion and well worth trying out, but it is no substitute for a War production spirit. Past experience indicates that this sort of innovation starts well, and then slides back into the old habit, and it is quite likely that the net result after a few weeks would be to add a further ten minutes to the time already lost to production. (See previous note on five mins. washing time allowed in the Machine Shop.)—(*Works Manager.*)

with a jerk, leans with her elbows on the bench. Sits thus, gazing in front of her, doing nothing. 2 mins.

10.15 a.m. Feels for lunch packet in cardboard box and fetches out two sandwiches. Works sporadically while she eats them, thus losing about three minutes altogether. 3 mins.

11.10 a.m. Puts the work she has just finished up on to the rack, and instead of bringing down a new one at once, she bends over the bench, arranging some tiny nuts she is working with in patterns of stars and crosses. They fit together very nicely, and she extends the pattern further and further, till there are no more nuts. Shuffles them together again, and reaches with a yawn for a new lot of work. 4 mins.

11.30 a.m. Has turned round on her chair, and is looking eagerly round the other side of the room for a particular girl her neighbour is talking to her about. 1 min.

11.45 a.m. Running the screwdriver idly up and down the cracks in the bench. 1 min.

11.50 a.m. Goes to cloakroom. 3 mins.

After this she works continuously until twenty-five past twelve when everyone starts to get ready to go.

Now, the point of this is that this girl has spent a total of *thirty-one minutes* doing something other than working; and yet, with one or two exceptions, nothing she has done could be picked on by a charge-hand or foreman as against the rules. She has not been knitting or reading; and she has talked rather less than most of the others. Between whiles she has worked well and efficiently, and has turned out all that was expected of her for the morning. She herself has no feeling of having idled away any of her time.

The moral is this. Since (short of having a foreman standing behind every chair) this sort of thing is absolutely inevitable during a long stretch of work, it would be just as sensible to have an official ten-minute break in the middle (very much less than the thirty minutes she is taking anyway), and thus reduce the unofficial wasting of time. In fact it would be more sensible, because an *official* ten minutes at a definite time that one can look forward to has a much more refreshing effect than an unofficial ten minutes (or even half an hour) taken casually, and mainly unconsciously.

It is probably useless to try and reduce this kind of wasting time by mere multiplication of prohibitions—forbidding talking, etc. Some attempt of this sort has been made to prevent time being wasted in the cloakrooms. No mirrors are provided, and there is a large notice put up, saying:

> "This cloakroom is to be used for essential purposes only. This does not include hairdressing, etc."

These obstacles have not, of course, the slightest effect on the amount of time people spend on doing their hair. It merely means that they do it in a rather slow and awkward manner with a pocket mirror. And even if it was possible to prevent the girls doing their hair during working hours, what would be gained? They would merely spend a similar amount of time yawning, fiddling with screws, or rearranging their handbags, and probably feel less stimulus for starting work again as well.

All this, of course, merely reinforces what has been proved a thousand times, by industrial psychologists and others—that human beings simply do not maintain a concentrated effort over a long period of time, and that the answer to this is not to blame the human beings, but to shorten the lengths of time. Or else, of course, to accept in good part the fact that the level of concentration will not be very high.[1]

(iii) ABSENTEEISM

The record of actual absenteeism is not bad; it is barely ten per cent (for all reasons), considerably lower than most factories in the district. Such as there is, other than for illness, is mainly of a pretty aimless kind; going to dances and then waking up too late in the morning to catch the bus, and so on. There is probably more purposeful absenteeism in the Assembly than in the machine shop. Here people are more inclined to make definite plans, like going away for the weekend on Friday night, and so missing Saturday morning's work.

But on the whole, far more time is probably wasted by dawdling inside the factory than ever by taking days off.

As in the case of other kinds of slacking, there is no pressure of public opinion against it. Girls will come in on Monday morning and describe to the whole bench just how they managed

[1] I cannot agree with this point of view under War conditions. M.-O. refers to the necessity for an emotional stimulus; surely the War itself, if "put over" in the right manner, provides just that stimulus. (This appears to be the case in Russia from all one hears.) This is the very crux of the whole problem of Wartime production from the personal angle, and is discussed in the Appendix—(*Works Manager*).

to get off on Saturday, and just what lies they are proposing to tell to the foreman, and receive nothing but sympathy and interest from their hearers, mixed with a certain amount of envy.

(iv) CASH INCENTIVES

It takes a long time for most factory managements to realise that men's and girls' attitudes to earning money are fundamentally different. To a man, to earn a good wage is a basic necessity; on this his own and his family's prestige and social position depends. To a large number of girls, however, the money is mainly pocket-money; the job merely a way of filling in time and meeting friends until she gets married. Thus incentives and deterrents in the form of bonuses and fines have always had a much weaker hold over girls than over men, even in peace time, and their power is even less now, when many of the girls don't even want to have the job at all, but have been forced to come into it.

The girls in this factory are no exception. Pay for a full week's work, with overtime, is about £2 15*s.*, but it is usually possible to leave early (at half-past five) on at least one night a week; thus losing, of course, two or three shillings overtime. But practically never did any of the girls think of this as a reason for *not* taking time off, if they could see any way of wangling permission. Similarly, when the question of Saturday afternoon work was under discussion. It had been proposed (and the proposal was later adopted) that Saturday afternoon work should be abolished, and that instead, overtime on Friday should be made compulsory (formerly work had stopped at five-thirty on Fridays and at five on Saturdays). This change meant the loss of the Saturday afternoon overtime pay, which is considerably more than that for Friday evenings. Yet in all the discussions which this proposal roused, one practically never heard any reference to the loss of money involved from any of the girls. They talked eagerly about all the things they would be able to do on Saturday afternoons; the shopping, walks, cinemas; some of them, too, talked about all the things they *wouldn't* be able to do on Friday evenings. Never was the cut in the pay packet mentioned as the primary factor. The men, meanwhile, had noticed that first of all, and many of them were complaining that it was done deliberately as a method of lowering wages. To them, that was the important point. To the girls, the important point was how it would affect their leisure.

Because of this attitude, money incentives are much less effective here than a management accustomed to employing men can easily realise. A penalty, like suspension, holds no terrors for the average girl. To a man, it is a shattering humiliation to have to go home and say that he is suspended for three days because of some piece of misbehaviour, and will be bringing no money home for that time; and then to spend those three days lounging about at home watching his wife economise to make up for it. But to a girl it is little more than a holiday and a big joke. Her father and brothers will laugh at her, and say: We told you so; women are no good in factories. And she will have to do without her Saturday shopping expedition. But to make up for it she will have three days in which to go to dances and get up late; which is something approaching her idea of heaven.

In the same way it is unlikely that any scheme for piece-work, or bonuses for extra work, would have a big effect on output. Certainly bonuses in the form of money would have nothing like the effect of bonuses in the form of leisure. If a girl was told that if she finished a certain amount by a certain time, then she could go home, she would probably work half again as fast as she does at present. And as a matter of fact a scheme approaching to this is to be started shortly; if a given bench finishes its set work for the week on Friday evening, then they don't have to come in on Saturday morning. We did not see this scheme actually working, but the proposal for it was greeted with great enthusiasm. Again, nobody was worrying about whether Saturday morning's pay would be docked or not under this scheme.[1]

(v) WORKERS' ORGANISATIONS

The influence of these on the female side of the factory is practically negligible. There are, as a matter of fact, vestiges of some Trade Unions, and there is a Works Committee, which is supposed to represent the views of the workers at managerial conferences. But we did not meet any of the ordinary girls at the benches who had ever considered any of them; if they had heard of the Works Committee, it was simply as a meaningless pair of words that sometimes appeared on notices. Interest

[1] Unfortunately it has been found impossible to introduce this scheme on account of objections raised by the Unions concerned, arising out of the Essential Work Order under which Saturday morning is considered as basic time which must be paid for as long as the employee is *available* for work. A possible variant may be introduced for Friday evenings—(*Works Manager*).

in anything of this sort did not start until considerably higher up in the factory than the workbench. Members of these organisations were some of them aware of this total lack of interest in their activities, and were worried by it. Others took the rather bewildering view that the factory was full of hostility towards them, fostered by a malicious opposition. It is difficult to understand how they got this impression, in view of the almost total unawareness of their existence among the rank and file.[1]

As a matter of fact, no one is to blame for this lack of interest. The whole attitude of the girls to their life and work here precludes the possibility of effective organisation; they are simply not interested enough in anything which happens or doesn't happen within the factory walls to bother with demands or explicit grievances of any sort. It is all part of the general apathy about life and work here.

(vi) FUNDAMENTAL: SOCIAL

These then are the facts as We saw them. we have made a few suggestions about how this, that, or the other might be improved. But this is not important. The basic trouble with this factory (and with many others too) is one which lies quite outside the scope of miscellaneous tinkering with conditions and regulations. It lies at the very roots of this country's attitude to its wartime life. The war is regarded (by many young working girls) with mainly negative emotions. The cardinal virtue is the negative one of endurance; endurance of danger; endurance of a distasteful job; endurance of shortages. And because the war has been put across with complete success as something to be endured (and after twenty years of anti-war emotion this was almost the only way in which it could be put across), not as something to be plunged into with zest and enthusiasm, this attitude of endurance is the one which people primarily bring to all the changes in their personal lives which the war has caused. They regard their new lives, not as an exciting adventure, full of new personal and social possibilities, but as something to be put up with until

[1] The Works Representative Committee is elected annually by departmental secret ballot. Employees joining the Company after election can take little interest under the circumstances, but representatives of the workers complain that once they have been elected there is very little interest in their activities on the part of rank and file. Many of the matters taken to foremen or to the Welfare Department should properly be routed through the worker's representative, but this does not happen. The Committee is now being expanded into a "Joint Production Consultative and Advisory Committee".—(*Works Manager*).

at last the peace life can be taken up again. The ambition that keeps girls going is not the hope of achieving something in the new life, but the hope that the peace will return soon. So far from wanting to make good under present conditions, the all-absorbing hope is that present conditions and all appertaining to them will, as soon as possible, have vanished, never to be thought of again.

This attitude makes it difficult for real social units to be formed, in or out of work. The attention of all the individuals is firmly focused on the social units to which they belonged before the war, no matter that these may be disintegrating; and they have no attention to spare for anything else. And without some sort of social cohesion it is impracticable to infuse a spirit of enthusiasm (or, indeed, of anything else) into a given group of people. Without this cohesion, no propaganda, however skilful, no smoothing out of grievances, however wise, will ever have more than trivial effect. When people begin to feel that they *belong* to their new social groups, that the new groups are personally important to them, then, and only then, will the ground be prepared for raising such storm of enthusiasm as will make arguments about a ten or a twelve-hour day sound like a meaningless quibble.

APPENDIX

by the WORKS MANAGER

DURING THE COURSE of observation which formed the subject of these notes, the general question of national, and included in the national the worker morale, became very much a topic of public discussion. Time wasting, absenteeism and so forth occupied a fair amount of space in the National Press. Hitherto there would appear to have been a conspiracy of silence in respect of such manifestations.

It must be confessed that as Manager of this somewhat isolated factory, I was almost as isolated from what was happening in the rest of the country and in other factories, as the workers themselves, and tended to feel that what I termed (for want of a better word) "lack of morale", was peculiar to my own organisation. The realisation that this was not so, but that it formed part of a much wider and National problem, while bringing some slight measure of relief from the purely personal angle, only transferred the problem to a different plane; the factory was still part of the National War Effort, and hence something still had to be done about it.

I have exchanged notes .with persons very much concerned with morale in the Services, particularly the Army, and from this very general aspect one outstanding feature emerges, that is, it is not possible for any prolonged period of time to raise the level of morale in a particular factory materially higher than that of its environment. A quotation from an article by Stephen Spender in *The New Statesman and Nation* of June 13th, on the question of disinterested War workers, is worth recording:

> "Men in the factories, the Army, the Civil Defence, work, but without a sense that they are sharing the responsibilities of the war. On the contrary, their great consolation is to feel that they are not responsible. At a discussion on the loss of Malaya amongst firemen, the men talked with a certain satisfaction about the hopeless incompetence of the 'ruling class' and the 'bosses'. . . . Convinced that they cannot do anything, they take the satisfaction of the impotent in the guilt, and indeed, to-day, the punishment, incurred by the potent ruling class. . . . Another reason is their feeling that they are uneducated. The way in which they are gradually awakening from the lethargy and despair of the past twenty

years is in a growing demand for education of various kinds. Above all, what is required is education in citizenship, to acquaint them with the kind of problem likely to arise in the next five years."

The extent to which "Pep Talks", visits to warships and aircraft, and other stimulants of a like nature raises morale is of little consequence in the long run, when the background of the War itself was long one of continual retreats or strategic withdrawals, bearing the implication that in spite of the efforts put forward to make the arms and equipment, it was either not good enough compared with the enemy's, or not being used correctly.

These are the conclusions arrived at without any thinking, and the effect was particularly noticeable throughout industry after the escape of the *Scharnhorst* and *Gneisenau.* There was a general atmosphere of "What is the use?" What appears to be wanted is a National consciousness that each is part of the greater whole, that each has a definite stake in winning the war, and that every person, however indirectly connected with the War Effort, is part of an essential War machine.

In my opinion, the lack of consistency in Government propaganda has resulted in the absence of such a consciousness. Not until Russia was invaded in June, 1941, did any real desire to get on with the job make itself apparent among the workers, and then only amongst that section who were politically minded or unconsciously attracted to the Russian experiment, with its implication of workers' control. Particular note was taken of the effect of Russia's entry into the war in this factory. Among a few of the older men with an industrial background, evacuees from London mainly, there was a definite quickening of spirit. An immediate tendency to want to say to the Management, "Look here, how can we help increase output?" Unfortunately among the large mass of employees there was only one noticeable reaction; that was a feeling of relief that Hitler had gone East instead of West, which meant a further respite and the possibility of Hitler getting bogged. Politically, Russia's advent into the War on our side was as of much consequence as if it had been some insignificant South American State. Such a result is only natural in a country atmosphere where the working classes tend to be less politically conscious, less well-educated, and less interested in the outside world than the townsman, and the very factor, i.e. Russia joining the Allies, which has tended to raise worker morale more than anything else, was of no help in my particular case.

In his book *People in Production,* Mr. Tom Harrisson makes an important point of the fact that the private ownership of industry makes it very difficult for the worker to take that direct War-time viewpoint and feel himself actually part of the War machine. I personally incline to this point of view, but surveys undertaken in nationally owned Ordnance Factories show morale therein to be as low as, and often lower than, in privately-owned industry.

The problem is far more complicated than could be dealt with by such expedients as nationalisation, etc. The time factor comes into it, but above it all there is no escape from the inevitable conclusion that it behoves factory managements to do everything in their power to remove complaints, make conditions as comfortable as possible, and provide for their workers as congenial a background for hard work as can possibly be devised. Beyond that the problem is a national one and can only be tackled nationally.

Events like Dunkirk put a spurt into the nation which does not last. The recent 1,000-bomber raids on Germany are the best tonic War Industry has received for many a year, but until the whole of the population really gets down to the job of fighting and winning this war, there will always be slackness on the part of the worker, as evidenced by absenteeism, lavatory-mongering, petty strikes, and manifested in other sections of the population in Black Market operations, evasion of quotas, illegal use of petrol, luxury feeding, and the like.

The accusation can be made that this is merely trying to get rid of a management problem by putting the blame on to the Government, but it is a conviction at which I have arrived, after very careful study, and the remarkable piece of observing reported in this survey has helped in no small way. Such surveys are invaluable to industrial managements, and while there is always the danger that an observer may be misunderstood and regarded as a "spy", I regard this new technique as being one of the most useful aids to understanding and efficiency ever made available to managements.

NOTE ON MACHINE SHOP

by the LABOUR MANAGER

THE MACHINE SHOP has always been the problem department of the factory. It is bound to be so by the uninteresting nature of the work as described by Mass-Observation. It tended to attract a more irresponsible type of employee and, what is worse has made more irresponsible those of a higher degree of intelligence or responsibility drafted into the department.

One of the most interesting suggestions made by M.-O. is the necessity for an emotional stimulus; this has been provided indirectly in the most successful way. During the period under survey the Machine Shop was largely staffed by female workers in the daytime and male labourers at night. It was decided, in order to economise in male labour, to dispense with the male night shift, expand the number of female operatives, and split them between day and night, alternating shifts each month. Within a week of this arrangement output began to soar, time wasting became obviously reduced, and a much better spirit became evident. The results in terms of efficiency showed that within a period of one month output was doubled.

Investigations were immediately undertaken to find out exactly how this had come about, and it was found that working on a night shift provided to those so engaged just that stimulus and sense of romance necessary to take a real interest in the job. Working during the day is just drudgery, but to turn up at work at eight o'clock in the evening when everybody else is going home definitely gives a sense of superiority of sacrifice, and resultant sense of satisfaction at doing a real job.

The night shift would come down the factory drive, six or seven girls arm in arm shouting "Good morning" to everybody, and conversely would go off in the morning shouting "Good night" to those arriving for day shift. Nobody ever saw the day shift coming to work with the same glee with which the night shift comes on. This was immediately noticed, possibly subconsciously, by the girls working on day shift, and questions began to be asked, "When are we going on nights?" They obviously felt they were missing something and wanted to cash in on the glamour surrounding girls working nights.

At the end of a month the shifts were reversed, and they have now worked two full periods of day and night each, and output is still up. Whether it will remain so when Winter comes, or whether it will die down when the novelty of working at night time wears off, remains to be seen, but the stimulus thus provided, albeit unconscious, had a far greater result than any increase in wages or any external event connected with the War, and is an interesting pointer.

Later Note—The stimulus of shift working appears to be wearing off, but a steady level is being maintained, much above the previous one-shift figures.

A NOTE TO READERS

We hope you have enjoyed this Cresset Library edition and would like to take this opportunity to invite you to put forward your suggestions about books that might be included in the series.

The Cresset Library was conceived as a forum for bringing back books that we felt should be widely available in attractively designed and priced paperback editions. The series themes can be loosely described as social, cultural, and intellectual history though, as you can see from the list of published titles at the front of this book, these themes cover a broad range of interest areas.

If you have read or know of books that fall into this category which are no longer available or not available in paperback, please write and tell us about them. Should we publish a book that you have suggested we will send you a free copy upon publication together with three other Cresset Library titles of your choice.

Please address your letter to Claire L'Enfant at:-

Century Hutchinson
FREEPOST
London
WC2N 4BR

There is no need to stamp your envelope.

We look forward to hearing from you.

THE CRESSET LIBRARY